Gayle Smerdon believes in people. As an experienced Learning & Organisational Development practitioner, she knows that when people are given the right environment and support, they have vast capability just waiting to emerge.

Working in the government and not-for-profit sectors, Gayle helps learners, teams and workplaces to discover their ONE THING – whatever it is – and supports them in achieving it.

With a PhD in the Social Sciences and a Grad. Dip. in Psychology, Gayle is deeply fascinated by people and the cultures of meaning they create. She speaks and writes about workplace cultures and coaches the curious and committed.

www.gaylesmerdon.com
www.linkedin.com/in/gayle-smerdon/

Also by Gayle Smerdon PhD

iDevelop: *How to take charge of your professional development by becoming a conscious learner*

The Janice Chronicles: *The adventures of two everyday people, doing ONE THING deep*

www.gaylesmerdon.com/the-janice-chronicles

DO ONE THING
AND DO IT DEEP

How to focus and energise your workplace

Gayle Smerdon PhD

BROADCAST

First published in 2021 by Gayle Smerdon
www.gaylesmerdon.com

A catalogue record for this work is available from the National Library of Australia

ISBN: 978-0-6489053-4-9 (Paperback)
ISBN: 978-0-6489053-5-6 (Ebook)

Produced by Broadcast Books, www.broadcastbooks.com.au
Cover and text design by Seymour Design, seymourdesign.net
Typeset by Seymour Design
Author photographs by Alise Black, Alise Black Photographic Studio
Printed by IngramSpark

To all my mentors, friends and colleagues who steadfastly carried a belief in me when I wasn't convinced I could.

And especially to my mum, because I am not sure when I will get around to writing that detective story you wanted.

CONTENTS

To pay attention, this is our endless and proper work.[1]

MARY OLIVER

PREFACE

Do not try to do everything. Do ONE THING well.[2]

STEVE JOBS

Where we choose to focus our attention shapes our world.

At work, we can find ourselves overwhelmed with frenetic busy-ness or underwhelmed by an inability to make decisions and implement anything. Sometimes these two states happen simultaneously. Each can leave us without a sense of clarity or feeling disengaged from the type of purposeful work that sustains a healthy organisation and its people.

Often the strategies used in organisations to harness the attention of their people are undervalued, unrealised or simply ineffectual. However, boosting efforts to focus all players on achieving a single meaningful objective can lead to a thriving workplace and an organisation fulfilling its potential. So what do we do to make this happen?

We need to do ONE THING and do it deep.

In this book, I don't tell you what your ONE THING should be. Instead, I offer tools to help an organisation harness the wisdom of its employees, customers and leaders. Then, together with your people, you can determine what that ONE THING will be for your workplace. Realising what that ONE THING is will make the difference between how your organisation functions now and how it needs to operate to secure the wellbeing of its people and its sustainability into the future.

Now this ONE THING you identify will be guided by your purpose. But determining this ONE THING doesn't mean everyone in your organisation will end up doing the same thing, the 'only' thing, all at the same time like automatons. Instead, your ONE THING will be the guiding principle for everyone to work by, creating better engagement, wellbeing and success – however you measure it – for your organisation, as a whole. This principle can manifest in different ways. It could incorporate a few themes or concepts already within your organisation, or it can flourish differently across each area and allow for local expression. And, you can always adjust this ONE THING over time to keep it relevant.

By using the concept of ONE THING to capture and direct everyone's attention, valuable energy can be positively refocused to reinvigorate the culture of your organisation. To do that successfully, your organisation's ONE THING needs to:

- be meaningful to the group and in service of the work

- engage people in identifying and building its success

- account for individual or local difference by engaging people in multiple ways

- allow sufficient time for those resistant to change to see its inherent value.

Embracing these points is doing ONE THING *deep*.

In the process of doing ONE THING deep, both employees and leaders come to see themselves as agents of change. They feel empowered to be curious and seek to identify, understand and address the challenges and opportunities that inevitably arise in the workplace. With each person working together within the frame of a single objective and, supported by their colleagues and leaders in an environment designed for success, the organisation's culture will flourish.

In this book, we'll cover the information you'll need to help you harness the attention of your organisation and its people. Here's a run-down of what to expect.

In **Part 1: Doing ONE THING** we examine the experiences and consequences of three types of workplaces:

- **The Every-THING workplace** – where too much is happening at once

- **The No-THING workplace** – where it's impossible to make anything happen

- **The ONE THING workplace** – where a single focus of attention creates a more positive and effective workplace environment.

In **Part 2: Doing it DEEP** we discover that while there are different ways to do ONE THING, doing it deep is often overlooked in organisations. And while deep is not always what's needed, there can be substantial damage caused by a focus on short-term goals and quick fixes. In this section, we look at how the Principles of Deep can help to overcome these issues.

In **Part 3: Now you do it** we take our principles and look at how to practice them. You'll learn the traps to avoid, ways to get this right, and ideas for a constructive approach for implementing your ONE THING. You'll dive into the culture of your organisation by examining the current **beliefs** – beliefs that will help to define your ONE THING; the **structures** that support them; and **agency** across the organisation. This focus will help you to realise undiscovered opportunities and identify what's been holding your workplace back. With this vital information, you'll be able to determine and embrace what will drive your organisation's future success.

In **Part 4: Three Campaigns and ONE THING** we learn from three different campaign disciplines that, combined, will create a strong foundation for approaching your ONE THING deep. First, we outline the best and most ethical elements of a *political campaign* and show the critical role leadership plays in any change that impacts the workplace and its culture. Then we examine how *engagement campaigns* can teach us to utilise the skills and creativity of an organisation's greatest resource – its people. Finally, we focus on some key ideas from *marketing campaigns* that will help you create and share the right messaging for your ONE THING to foster broad engagement and ongoing support from all involved.

Lastly, in **Part 5: A *do*-ONE THING-*deep* Fable** we dive into the experience of someone who's about to run their first *do*-ONE THING-*deep* campaign. Told from the perspective of a leader who takes their leadership team and organisation on a *do*-ONE THING-*deep* journey, it demonstrates how concentrating on ONE THING can make a difference in any organisation.

By focusing our attention on what matters and applying the Principles of Deep, we can create a workplace where people not only feel that *what* they do matters, but that *they* matter. Feeling valued and sharing a common purpose helps to break down boundaries and build bridges. From my research and experience in this area, I believe that finding constructive and effective ways to connect people in a complex business environment can help us achieve the same outside of the workplace … and maybe even save the world.

Now *that* would be doing ONE THING deep.

What you stay focused on will grow.[3]

ROY T BENNETT

INTRODUCTION
THE PARADOX OF ONE THING

*If one is master of ONE THING and understands
ONE THING well, one has at the same time, insight
into and understanding of many things.*[4]

VINCENT VAN GOGH

I'm not sure when I first noticed, but I'm pretty sure it's been happening for a while now. I'm at home sitting on the couch, standing in a room, or simply walking about when I hear myself saying, 'Just do ONE THING'. And I do say it a lot. For instance:

- I say it when I'm not sure what to do next

- I say it when I'm feeling overwhelmed and trying to do too many things

- I say it when I've been distracted and need to refocus on what's important

- I say it when I need to kick-start my motivation

- I say it when I need to help someone else to focus.

While I'm not sure how this started in my personal life, I clearly remember the day I had an epiphany about doing ONE THING at work.

I was walking back to my desk in an office located on the 23rd floor of a building in the CBD. It overlooked some familiar Melbourne landmarks: the solid sandstone parliament buildings, the lush Treasury Gardens, the metropolitan trains going to and from Flinders Street Station, the Melbourne Cricket Ground and the broader sports precinct. But I wasn't noticing any of these just at that moment. I had come to a standstill in the middle of the floor and was busy contemplating a paradoxical revelation. And aren't they always the best sort to have?

I had just come from a meeting where I was given a new project. It would have a significant impact on a lot of people and processes across the organisation. There was a pretty tight timeframe and not a lot of detail about expectations. Still, that was what I was paid for – landing ideas. It was my job to take my boss's giant thought bubbles and ground them.

But this one felt different. There was no good rationale for doing it, not even a barely okay one. It didn't align with anything else we were doing and, from what I could make out, it only had a tenuous link to our overall strategic plan.

Plus, I already had a lot – like, a *lot* – of projects on the go and was spinning plates to keep them all happening. If I were to take on this new project, I wasn't sure I'd be able to keep my existing ones from crashing to the ground. Sure, they could be pushed out or stopped, but I was worried about the impact that would have on the trust and engagement I had built up with stakeholders, the progress made to date and the momentum that was building. I feared that by shifting my focus to something new, my other projects would be irreparably damaged and a lot of good work and goodwill would be lost.

As I was standing there, my mind racing, I caught myself feeling overwhelmed. I took a deep breath, sighed and said to myself, 'Can we just do ONE THING?'.

Then I burst out laughing as I recalled an experience at my previous workplace.

That organisation had proved to be very different kettle of fish. I had tried very hard to get projects implemented, but it was impossible to get anything up and running. There were many meetings and hours of planning but nothing was ever rolled out. There was always a reason not to do something 'just yet'. Or maybe we 'needed a new approach'. Or someone else had to approve the idea as well, before any work could progress. In that role, I would find myself sick with frustration and pleading with my boss, 'Can we just do ONE THING?'.

But back to my epiphany. My laughter, which was attracting a little attention, came from my realisation that I had said 'Just do

ONE THING' in situations that were polar opposites. At my old workplace, this phrase would pop out of my mouth or echo in my mind because nothing was happening, except for me experiencing a sense of ennui and hopelessness. In my new workplace, there was so much going on that I felt overwhelmed. Not only was this amusing, but it made me very, very curious.

Over the next few years, I became sensitive to the concept of 'doing ONE THING' and realised that it was following me around at work. Noticing where there were ONE THINGs – or more usually, ONE THING-shaped holes – became a bit of an obsession for me. I started to think about what ONE THING meant in different workplaces and I wanted to delve a little deeper into the Every-THING workplace and the No-THING workplace. And I began to wonder what exactly was this ONE THING anyhow?

Let's start there first.

The nature of ONE THING

This is a little embarrassing, really. When it comes to telling people what a ONE THING is, I can't really say. I have a certain reticence describing it. I think it's because I don't really like telling people what they should do – although my sister might disagree with that. Instead, I like helping people, teams and organisations uncover what matters to them, then I like to help them find a way to make that happen. And if we look at it this way, a ONE THING can be many different things because it's whatever you say it is. It's also not uncommon that a ONE THING might be more than just *one* thing. Sounds tricky? Perhaps starting with a classic example of how this works will help.

For many years, the British Rowing Eight failed to win Olympic gold for the UK – since 1912, in fact. Sheesh![5] So they came up with a saying – in this case, a question – to help them focus their attention on what really mattered. Any decision or action they made would be tested against the question, 'Will it make the boat go faster?' When the answer was 'Yes', they explored the idea broadly, deeply and persistently. When the answer was 'No', they would let it go or give the decision to someone else. They were concerned with only ONE THING, and their focus and diligence were rewarded by the team winning gold in the 2000 Sydney Olympics.

So what is this ONE THING?

ONE THING is best defined as **an overarching idea for focusing collective actions that can demonstrate change**. A ONE THING can be identifying an opportunity, accepting a challenge, something you want to do (or be) more or less of, or something you want to do better in some way.

You can do ONE THING at many different levels, including:

- **An individual level** – with a focus on professional development and performance

- **A team level** – to build connection, effectiveness and productivity

- **A leadership team level** – to focus on how the team lead together

- **A departmental or cohort level** – to consolidate how your department or profession works using specialised skills and knowledge, or working with particular types of clients

- **An organisational level** – to focus on building a positive workplace culture and delivering your organisation's overall strategy.

This book is predominantly focused on how ONE THING works at scale in an organisation or department. Its main aim is to assist leaders and leadership teams to harness the power of their people's attention. However, the principles of doing ONE THING deep can be used by anyone working in an organisational context, and will be especially useful to those involved in change programs, project management and communications.

Now when some people first hear about doing ONE THING they are concerned it means that this is the only thing they will do all day long, together, and simultaneously, with everyone else in the workplace. They picture the organisation working like a row of automatons, arms synchronised in motion on an endless production line. This makes the concept of ONE THING feel limiting, a barrier to innovation and productivity. But nothing could be further from the truth.

ONE THING can be like an umbrella – an idea that makes sense of multiple things that are going on. Focusing on ONE THING involves bringing information together so that it is easier to grasp. By doing so, your ONE THING becomes a guiding principle, a manifesto that can act as a catalyst for a range of actions. Recording it, writing it down, making it visible and sharing it has a strong impact.

ONE THING

A   B   C   D

Whatever the impetus is for an organisation to focus on ONE THING – an issue, in response to survey data, the opportunity to develop the team or to better align initiatives – it helps to have a cohesive story to tell. Clearly articulating your ONE THING offers a way to talk about what's happening and makes the progress of your ONE THING tangible. Your people will understand the steps being taken and the role they play. In addition, there is the opportunity to shine a light on what's working well and share the learnings from what could have gone better. That sort of transparency is transformative.

Aspects of your ONE THING will set it apart from the everyday. For example, it might involve specific events, programs and engagement that capture the attention and imagination of your people. In general, though, your ONE THING will be found in the warp and weft of your organisation's daily work life. It's not an added extra but a lens, a mindset, a way of seeing and working that benefits everything you and your people do.

ONE THINGs are most often targeted at the 'how' of work, but they come from the 'why' you work – your purpose, mission and vision. They are situated in the context of the 'what' of your work – the industry, business and individual roles. Focusing your workplace becomes about how you do this ONE THING better. How do you skill, engage, inspire and support your people to do and be their best? And when they are, you move to the next ONE THING.

Let's do a thought experiment

Write a list of a few things you think your organisation could be doing better. Maybe it's your current workplace, or one that you have previously worked in, or even a social or community group you're involve with. It's just an experiment so have a go at it. If the organisation were to get some – or even ONE – of these things right, it would have a major positive impact on achieving its vision, delivering its strategy and living the organisation's values. It could help that organisation create great products, serve their clients well and make it a better place for people to work.

Go on, make a list. I am sure you can get a few options down without too much effort at all.

I recall many get-togethers with colleagues that turned into SALT (Self-Appointed Leadership Team) meetings. We would happily identify everything that wasn't working with the organisation and where the actual leaders were getting stuff wrong. We would come up with brilliant solutions – far superior, of course, to anything that was happening. (Yes, some people might call this whinging, but I think it's pretty normal and healthy, as long as it doesn't get out of hand.)

Now that you have your list, go through it and pick ONE idea. Focus on this ONE THING that is important to you. It can be a personal bugbear, or maybe it's something you think would be tricky – or pretty easy – to fix. As long as you care about it, that's all that matters.

Do you have ONE? Great. Now every time you read ONE THING in this book, try replacing it with the ONE you have identified. That way, you'll start to see how it's possible to make a real and significant change in your company or organisation.

Now let's get back to our Every-THING and No-THING workplaces before we dive deeper into the concept of ONE THING.

PART 1
DOING ONE THING

What we choose to focus on and what we choose to ignore – plays in defining the quality of our life.[6]

CAL NEWPORT

While a No-THING workplace and an Every-THING workplace may elicit the same plea from a frustrated worker (i.e., me) the experience of working in each one couldn't be more different.

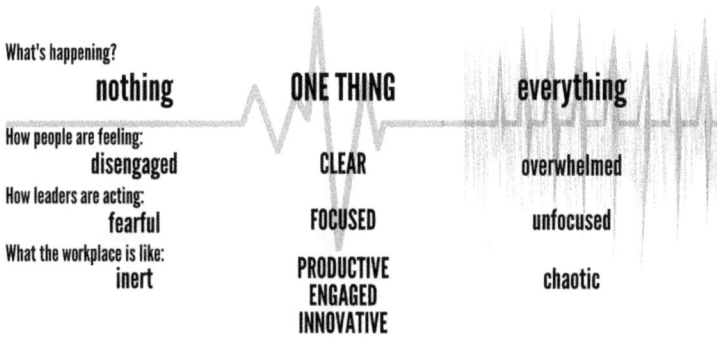

What's happening?		
nothing	ONE THING	everything
How people are feeling:		
disengaged	CLEAR	overwhelmed
How leaders are acting:		
fearful	FOCUSED	unfocused
What the workplace is like:		
inert	PRODUCTIVE ENGAGED INNOVATIVE	chaotic

When nothing is happening in a workplace, there is an undeniable sense of inertia. People feel disengaged and leaders are often fearful of taking action. At the other end of the scale, when everything is happening, there is a sense of chaos. People feel overwhelmed and leaders are unable to focus enough on anything to make a lasting difference.

But when the balance is right, the heart of the organisation beats to a ONE THING drum. There is a sense of positivity that creates a productive, engaged and innovative environment. People are clear about their roles and leaders are focused on the ONE THING that matters – whatever that might be for the organisation.

CHAPTER 1
THE EVERY-THING WORKPLACE

One who chases after two hares won't catch even one.[7]

JAPANESE PROVERB

Have you ever worked with a boss or leadership team that had a new idea every five minutes? The business is constantly looking to transform itself with what is described as 'an aggressive agenda of reform and innovation'. The organisation's wild enthusiasm for the new and the next means everyone is going full throttle on many fronts. Work is coming at you from all directions, with a tremendous sense of urgency and little sense of direction. With so much going on, it's hard to give any ONE THING sufficient attention.

You know you are in an Every-THING workplace because everyone is busy and they usually like to tell you how busy they are. I know I did. There's a certain sense of importance, a status about always being a bit too busy that remains stubbornly resistant to all our talk of work–life balance. But being so busy with everything has an uncanny knack of stealing away the significance of anything.

When I worked in an Every-THING workplace, I always felt a sense of dread as the end of the financial year approached because of the many looming deadlines. Each year, there would be a swathe of projects needing to be completed. The list of actions in the previous year's annual report – the ones that my team and I had been too busy to fully attend to during the year – would taunt me. Projects would be whooshed through to meet their (sometimes entirely arbitrary) deadlines.

And it wasn't only my team's projects to consider – there were everyone else's projects, too. Everyone with a line in the business plan had projects they had not had time to complete because they were also too busy. We often found ourselves awash with 'being engaged' over matters we'd never heard of before, and our time taken up with meetings, reporting and testing for more projects than you could poke a stick at.

I can't say my Every-THING workplace wasn't exciting at times. But eventually, it wore me and everyone else down. We were all left feeling overwhelmed.

Under pressure

Around 70 per cent of organisations struggle with employees becoming overwhelmed,[8] having too much work with too little time to do it in. In contemporary corporate life, this situation arises regularly.[9] Here are just some of the many reasons why this can happen:

- The digital distractions of notifications and emails relentlessly ping into our consciousness. We are required to attend many, many meetings, even if we're not really sure why. It's estimated that at many companies, the proportion of time spent in meetings, on the phone and responding to emails hovers around 80 per cent, leaving little time to do substantive work.[10]

- Projects and initiatives multiply like rabbits in springtime.[11] Not only are they more numerous,[12] but we are required to collaborate more. Being a good corporate citizen by supporting projects and our co-workers is beneficial, but if we do this too much, the additional workload can carry a personal and professional burden.[13]

- With an explosion in the volume of and access to new research, information, opinions and practices,[14] there is so much more to know about our areas of expertise. It's hard to keep up with the latest thinking.

- We are working with less support and have greater reliance on self-service for systems and administration,[15] which may not always be the best use of our time and resources.

- There can be an expectation to be 'on' and available outside work hours,[16] although in some countries this is changing.

In essence, as we try to stay up to date, while working on multiple activities with less support for more hours of the day, we are constantly distracted and unable to focus.

Participants in a recent study reported on the costs to their health from overwork. These included:

heart attacks and strokes, disrupted sleep and related forgetfulness, unexplained hives, and other ills ... an inability to muster the energy to exercise and to prepare healthy meals, and work pressures that prompted them to smoke and drink more than they considered wise ... significantly higher levels of burnout, stress, and psychological distress (feeling sad, nervous, restless, hopeless, worthless, and that everything is an effort).[17]

In an Every-THING workplace, there is an increased risk of physical and psychological harm that can impact on individuals, teams and organisations.[18]

We clearly aren't built for this. The brain doesn't have endless capacity, and it is easily maxed-out in an Every-THING workplace. It turns out that we have limited attention, and we can't reliably do more than ONE THING at a time. With this in mind, let's take a closer look at attention and how its limits play out in Every-THING workplaces.

On attention

Everyone knows what attention is. It is the taking possession by the mind, in clear and vivid form, of one out of what seem several simultaneously possible objects or trains of thought. Focalization, concentration of consciousness are of its essence. It implies withdrawal from some things in order to deal effectively with others ...[19]

This quote by American philosopher and psychologist William James is perhaps the most referenced passage on the nature of attention. But we probably understand attention best through the oft-used metaphor of the spotlight. No matter how you think about it, for the most part we, as individuals, can only focus our spotlight of attention on ONE THING at a time, with a handful of exceptions to this rule (see under 'The myth of multitasking' in the next section).

And by saying 'Yes' to placing our attention in one spot, we say 'No' to everything else.

Paying the price

As Helen Garner, award-winning novelist and journalist, wrote:

I began to wonder why the verb that goes with 'attention' is 'to pay'. Is it a debt? A duty? A tax? An outlay of energy? Work seems to be involved in the phrase, or perhaps sacrifice. And what do we get back, if we pay it?[20]

There is a price when we pay attention, but it is both a cost and an investment. The cost is the energy we expend. The brain has a high consumption tax on attention. There is also the cost of possible lost opportunities, as there are many other things we will not be doing while focusing on this ONE THING. But the investment is in the potential benefits – and there are many – that we will gain from doing our ONE THING.

From a personal perspective, I admit it is taxing to focus on writing this book (and maybe more so reading it, who knows?). After a while, my brain starts to hurt. I can't sustain this activity for long periods without a break. Focusing on this, my current ONE THING, also means I am not catching up with friends, shopping, cooking carbonara, cleaning the garage, exercising (yeah, right), getting other work done or having a haircut. But I enjoy seeing ideas emerge from the scratchings I put down on the page and can see meaning arise out of the assembly of words. This process brings me joy.

Our lives are shaped by where we put our attention. Attention determines how you experience the world. It can't be otherwise. Where you put your focus right now will shape your thinking and what you do.

As I write this, I am well engaged with putting some concepts into words. Sitting here, I am unaware of the many things going on around me until I broaden my focus, or they become salient enough to push through and distract me. When I expand my attention, I notice the swoosh of the dishwasher, hear the happy crunching sounds the cat makes while eating from her bowl, and feel the sensation of sitting on the couch. At times, I am tempted to stop writing by the lure of other activities. The telly in the corner reminding me that watching another episode of my latest favourite show might be good. A seductive little bar of chocolate in the kitchen gently whispering my name ... I salivate at the thought. I am aware of them, but I am engaged in my writing so my attention is here – trying to craft something that will hopefully one day be a book.

Depending on what we are doing, our brains are quickly exhausted, and we can only sustain attention for a short time. You are probably aware that the brain has a two-speed engine and slightly faulty transmission. One of the systems in our brain acts automatically and uses very little of our limited energy. We rely on it to breathe and recall what that thing over there is with four legs and a base that we can sit on. We can't reinvent everything in the world every time we see it. That would be absurd, exhausting and we would all still be living in caves. This handy automatic and inexpensive system holds our models of the world. It's really very useful most of the time.

The other equally valuable system in our brain deals with those things that are novel to us or need to be actively thought about and understood, such as multiplying 13 by 268, choosing which of these fridges I should buy, deciding not to yell at that jerk, or figuring out next year's budget. This system is a gas guzzler. Comparing the two, this one is the Pontiac Grand Prix (just google least fuel efficient car ever) to the other system's Toyota Prius. And bad news: in this system's world, there's always a fuel crisis.

The need to actively engage our attention is one sure way to plumb tucker out our brain. This is especially true for work that engages our executive functions, such as focusing, planning, prioritising, decision making, emotional regulation, and initiating and persisting with tasks. And that doesn't sound like anything we would be trying to do at work, does it? When we 'try to process too much information, we may feel the strain of overload because of the hard limit on our brain capacity'.[21]

The myth of multitasking

As well as not having a huge capacity, our brains aren't great at managing lots of things at once. Yes, we can multitask – we do it all the time. I can walk and breathe and carry my cup of tea downstairs. I can go for a run and listen to music, although that example is more hypothetical. Where the neural pathways are significantly different, we *can* do more than ONE THING at once. But you can't read a book and write an email at the same time. I can only listen to music that doesn't have understandable lyrics when working, otherwise, my brain is actively focused on trying to understand what is being sung rather than on what I'm meant to be reading or writing.

Whenever we need to focus our attention on more than ONE THING, we decrease the efficiency of our activities, sometimes dangerously so.

I'm pretty sure people are more aware of this now, because of our need to navigate multiple sources of digital media. As we talk on the phone while looking at something on our tablet device and watching telly, we like to think we are great multitaskers but we are fooling ourselves. We are switching our focus from one thing to another, or 'task switching'. Each time we task switch, we use more of the brain's limited energy supply.

While digital media is a popular way to think about this problem, it's not new. The scale and speed may be. But focus is and always has been needed in all walks of life. I'm sure my dad's thumb was aware of the cost of distraction – being constantly interupting by his daughter while he was hammering. But that's another sort of 'digital' issue.

Except for about 2 per cent of the population, the kind of multitasking ability we believe we possess is a myth.[22] Trying to do more than ONE THING at a time impacts your working memory[23] and is a real productivity killer.[24] One study found that 'a typical office worker gets only 11 minutes between each interruption, while it takes an average of 25 minutes to return to the original task after an interruption'.[25] No wonder it feels like we are getting nowhere. When we are constantly being distracted, it can impact our sense of accomplishment.[26] And that's not good for our wellbeing.

Organisational multitasking

Despite our human limitations, the Every-THING workplace rushes ahead with multiple priorities. With a 'Let's get everything done now' mindset and agendas as big as the whole outdoors, you have to admire the ambition and enthusiasm of this style of organisation. But there is a toll.

Multitasking is sometimes humourously described as the ability to stuff up several things at once. It's an apt analogy for the Every-THING workplace. When multiple incoherent initiatives – each with significant cultural, behavioural, procedural, financial and policy implications – are simultaneously unleashed on unsuspecting employees, no one wins. Like us, organisations can do a few things at once. But they cannot – and should not – multitask with the things that matter, particularly when doing so threatens to impact the culture, purpose, values or strategy of the organisation and the wellbeing of its people.

Acting on lots of new goals can be exciting – some of them may even be needed. But the kicker comes when it is time to implement them. People are already busy with their everyday work. Providing input to multiple initiatives and finding time to unlearn the old and learn the new is a rapid path to fatigue. And with targets, KPIs, strategic and business goals to meet, everyone can become completely overwhelmed. Unless, somehow, these tasks can all fit together as ONE THING.

When we see how things align, it becomes easier to overcome the two core problems of the Every-THING workplace: the inability to prioritise long-term gains and self-interested silos.

Long-term gains

Making room for what's important in an urgent world is not easy. Recognising our bias for short-term thinking is a good start. We are wired to notice what's near us in time and space.[27] In an organisational context, that means we tend to look at the next urgent problem, rather than thinking of the big picture. We need to adopt a mindset that is alert to this, but we first need to care. And that can be a more structural or political matter. For many organisations, the quick gains of a short-term approach often seem to outweigh the benefits of long-term thinking[28] – and not just in profits.

However, there are some great examples out there of successful companies that put employees, customers, communities and the environment first.[29] They focus on a clear purpose, live their values and work strategically to achieve their success. This requires being diligent about implementation and means leaders must say 'No' to what's unreasonable and unaligned to their organisation's guiding principles. This is how organisations avoid being overwhelmed by the corrosive effects of a short-term thinking.

Self-interested silos

When an organisation isn't clearly focused and aligned on ONE THING, leaders have a way of going off and doing their own THING. They may have good reasons, like meeting perceived gaps in strategy and execution, but sometimes it's more about ego. Avoiding sharing information and resources for the good of the whole business can have costly implications. A silo mentality can 'reduce efficiency in the overall operation, reduce morale, and may contribute to the demise of a productive company culture'.[30] Leaders and leadership teams need to check they are working for the organisation, not just for their division or their own personal agenda.

Unlike its people, we've given the Every-THING workplace our full attention. But what if too much work isn't the problem? Let's check out what's not happening in the No-THING workplace.

CHAPTER 2
THE NO-THING WORKPLACE

Work spares us from three great evils: boredom, vice and need.[31]

VOLTAIRE

Turns out, Voltaire might not have got this quite right. In Every-THING workplaces, there is a sense of hustle that can be exciting. Having lots to do makes you feel needed and important. But what happens when you are stuck in a workplace that feels like you are living the movie *Groundhog Day*?

In some organisations I have worked in, it felt as if nothing was ever happening. This sense of being stuck was physically, mentally, emotionally and professionally corrosive. At times, the inability of the organisation to do anything appeared to stem from risk-averse leaders and managers. There was no drive or vision for anything new, and everybody was concerned with covering their arse. Heads down, working on with a 'business-as-usual' attitude, no questions asked – there was no oxygen for anything new or different. It was like the genes for innovation, creativity and curiosity – and with them, the dream to improve what we did and how we did it – had been magically CRISPR-ed[32] away.

Don't get me wrong, there are excellent reasons for not doing things. But after a while working in a No-THING workplace, you realise this inaction is something more than reasonable caution and due diligence.

It's frustrating to have managers who love an idea, clearly see it's a business need, have the budget (or need none), only to have them say they want more time to think about it. Not once, but repeatedly. 'It's not the perfect thing'; 'It could go wrong'; 'Things are a bit busy right now'; 'It's not my idea so I don't want the responsibility'. These frequent excuses are extremely demoralising.

Everything suggested is stalled. More than one manager I worked with couldn't make a decision. There was always a reason to ponder every idea a little more, or they required more information. And then there were the ongoing requests for another meaningless revision. Uncertainty about the budget was never resolved, despite assurances that a lack of resources wasn't an obstacle to our resourcefulness. It was never quite the right time for a proposed project, or it needed to go to yet another committee or stakeholder group before approval could be granted. Or there was a last-minute 'refocus' for the project that meant a complete do-over was required.

Despite rigorously and frequently checking requirements, sharing progress, presenting the work in various ways and actioning feedback, rarely was a decision made about progressing the work. Instead, there was a lot of continued effort but no action and absolutely no progress.

Interestingly, research suggests that having too little to do can have a more significant negative impact on us than having too much to do. In one study, those experiencing overload rated their job satisfaction at 57 per cent. That's 8 per cent higher than those who felt they had too little to do.[33]

Feeling a bit bored now and again is not necessarily a bad thing. It can be a warning sign[34] that we need to refocus, reset goals and make something happen. To some degree, this is our responsibility. We might need to check our mindset and reframe our perspective. But in an environment where things are stagnating, and you feel repeatedly stymied around the most reasonable activities and changes, the acute frustration will eventually wear a body down. You can't understand why things aren't progressing, and you feel unseen and unheard.

From coaching sessions with clients, conversations with colleagues and personal experience, I've seen the devastating effects that being excluded from productive and meaningful work can have on people's self-esteem and mental wellbeing. It is a form of bullying.[35]

When nothing is happening, employees start feeling disengaged. The No-THING workplace saps their energy. The entropy that exists in organisations with such limited vision brings with it a keen sense of frustration. People feel that their skills are under-utilised, the work is without purpose and there is a lack of any opportunity to grow and develop. A downward spiral begins with a loss of confidence and, eventually, people stop trying altogether. And if they are unlucky or not careful, they – perhaps you – begin to fit right in. In this situation, those affected begin to demonstrate the learned helplessness and lack of autonomy that is the No-Thing-workplace norm. And this undermines self-worth, affects drive and motivation, and creates a sense of hopelessness that will stop employees from moving on and finding a workplace where they feel valued and able to contribute.

This sense of worthlessness infects employee performance, morale and retention and has impacts well beyond the workplace.[36] Along with immediate physical and psychological damage, there is evidence emerging that negative feelings and low self-worth increases the likelihood of more serious long-term consequences, including cognitive decline.[37] Aside from the personal cost, this sort of disengagement of an organisation's people is costly to the company's bottom line and the wellbeing of its workforce.

Organisational ennui

Presented with an opportunity to shift the business culture, some organisations retreat to the perceived safety of doing nothing. Let's look at why this might happen.

A suspicion of the work's value

Some leaders fail to see the strong connection between culture and business outcomes, both positive and negative. They are distracted by urgent issues and find it hard to keep the bigger picture in view and engage a more strategic mindset for solutions. They believe focusing on 'how we could work better' is difficult, time-consuming and ineffective compared to sticking with just doing 'what we do'. This is especially true when leaders have observed previous attempts at change that were unsuccessful, with the result that little value is placed on working to strengthen the organisation's culture and its people.

A problem with identifying what to do

As any number of consulting firms and leadership experts will attest,[38] there is increasing recognition of the need to focus on company culture. There are ongoing revelations in the media exposing the damage a poor culture can have on an organisation.[39] But even in organisations that are not wilfully blind or simply ignorant, a lack of confidence or the inability to identify and diagnose the real issues or seize opportunities can be a significant stumbling block to strengthening workplace culture. Faced with multiple options, the No-THING workplace finds the choices overwhelming. Unable to decide which salient problem to solve first, or how to approach the task, the organisation does nothing – and nothing changes.

Difficulty in implementing effectively

With competing agendas and interests, and different personalities in the mix, getting stuff done can be laborious. Without the right people, approach and energy, it can be hard to put a plan in place, marshal the resources, get engagement and build the necessary momentum. Some key reasons why organisations fail to implement positive changes include the lack of an overarching strategic plan, unrealistic goals and a lack of leadership.[40]

At times, there are good reasons not to do things. However, endlessly putting off taking action is a special kind of frustration for leaders, teams and employees. Continual inaction discourages people. Talented and productive employees will find opportunities elsewhere, and the organisation is left with a disgruntled, disengaged workforce made up of those who stay behind. Or as one of my bosses used to say, the eagles fly and the turkeys stay.

A special kind of nothing

There is ONE No-THING, or 'nothing', that I find regularly and particularly disappointing. It is the engagement/culture/climate/pulse/staff survey. Whatever it's called, it is rarely used well.

The survey is set up then promoted to the organisation's people, usually with all sorts of inducements because participation is low – gifts of iPads, coffee vouchers, etc. You know the drill. Once the survey is done, expensive, time-consuming reports are prepared and sent to leaders. And then ... nothing much happens. The link between what employees wrote in the survey about what mattered to them, any action that occurred in the organisation as a result and the impact those actions had overall are never spelt out. When no one closes the loop on an organisation's successes, it's no wonder employees don't bother taking part in the next survey.

A poorly used survey is like an expensive hamster wheel: it just goes around and around. There is no return on investment. People feel unheard and engagement is damaged. Yet the staff survey could be a useful catalyst for change. It could provide valuable insights into where best to focus people's energy and attention.

In short, it's an excellent resource for an organisation's next ONE THING.

CHAPTER 3
THE ONE THING WORKPLACE

You become what you give your attention to.[41]

EPICTETUS

Obviously, neither the No- nor the Every-THING situation is ideal. I have experienced the power of focused attention – of 'just doing ONE THING' in the workplace – in a couple of organisations, on a handful of projects, and with one or two managers. I've seen the value and know the potential for using it more often – it's transformative.

Identifying ONE THING that could act as a North Star that will set a clear purpose for a team or a whole organisation can make such a difference. This simple act of focus creates a sense of clarity and a feeling of calm excitement – which, okay, even sounds weird to me.

Where leaders align the intentions behind a complex range of activities and projects, it is easier for everyone to understand and master their role. It also makes working on what's important clearer. It simplifies the decisions about where to allocate resources that could support and develop people in the organisation. It gives leaders a sense of how to build and reflect on their leadership. People become engaged, productive and there is an increased sense of possibility. Doing ONE THING can transform a No-THING or Every-THING workplace into a more harmonious and productive enterprise – and that's when things really start to hum.

Energy follows attention. When you focus your people on ONE THING, you release a lot of momentum that flows in a single direction. Many organisations do attempt this, but only to a limited extent. They create a vision, mission statements, values and strategies, but mostly fail to harness their full potential and capture their people's attention.

Nice try

When fully deployed, carefully thought through and well-crafted, the ideas captured in the vision, values and strategies of an organisation are priceless. They can be used to engage hearts and minds, clarify expectations and support a positive culture. But usually, they don't. In my experience there tend to be four possible outcomes for these essential organisational expressions.

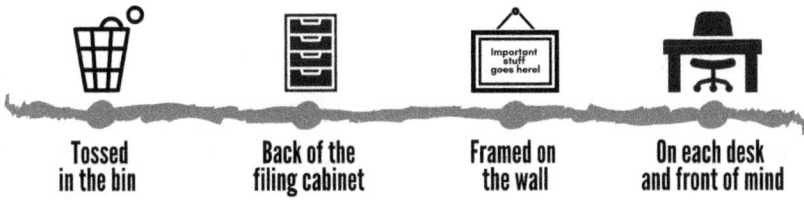

| Tossed in the bin | Back of the filing cabinet | Framed on the wall | On each desk and front of mind |

Tossed in the bin

Eventually, all frameworks and strategies go into the rubbish bin. At some point, they lose their value and need to be refreshed or started again from scratch. It's their very own circle of life, but sometimes it's a tiny, tiny circle – they may be binned before they've even had a chance to fly, and often for many of the same reasons they get 'filed'.

Back of the filing cabinet

Sometimes, these guiding ideas are created only to end up living at the very back of the filing cabinet's bottom drawer. Banished and forgotten, they are trapped in their basement prison like dark monsters or hidden treasures.

Maybe there were other immediate priorities, a crisis or a leadership change that distracted and delayed their implementation. Then when the time finally came to try again, momentum had been lost. In which case, it would require a significant effort to re-establish interest and commitment ... and possibly an organisational defibrillator.

Also, some people believe that once it's built, it's done. The next priority appears, and it's time to move on. With a lack of implementers in the organisation, people feel simultaneously overwhelmed by too many shiny new things and underwhelmed by having no understanding of how these ideas work or why they need to care about them. These ideas lose their lustre and sink further into the depths of the bottom drawer.

Framed on the wall

Ever walk into an organisation and see very admirable models, words and icons adorning the walls? You see the organisation's values, their mission statement and strategic priorities, yet when you look at the environment, facilities or the demeanour of employees, you think, *Huh? Really?*

These ideas have the appearance of an art installation, not lived beliefs. You may find yourself asking if the company has its feet and mouth aligned, because there's little evidence of it walking the talk. There's just lots of gorgeous yet hollow cultural expressions that are clearly endorsed but never reinforced.

On the desk and front of mind

Every now and again, organisations create something people feel is worth the effort, something they want to own that keeps its place on the desk and front of mind. This sort of idea will be relevant and meaningful. It will be **clear** (easy to understand), **simple** (easy to do) and **sticky** (easy to recall and share).

And that's what you want *your* ONE THING to be.

The missing question

In *The Advantage: Why organizational health trumps everything else in business*, Patrick Lencioni describes how each organisation needs to answer six critical questions to promote organisational health.[42] These include:

- Why do we exist? (The organisation's purpose, mission or vision)
- How do we behave? (The organisation's values)
- What do we do? (The basic definition of the business)
- How will we succeed? (What strategic plan is in place)
- Who must do what? (The roles required to make everything work).

While most organisations have some answer to these questions, Lencioni also asks a question that is often missing or dangerously undercooked, 'What is most important, right now?' That is, what is the organisation's single thematic goal, rallying cry, ONE THING?[43] Lencioni believes that understanding the ONE THING you and your organisation need to accomplish over the next however-many months has the most significant potential for impacting organisational health.

Taking our best intentions – the strategies, values and purpose of the organisation – and focusing them through a ONE THING lens can help us avoid the frustration of inertia and the feeling of being overwhelmed. Directing organisational attention to a common goal will not only release energy and the potential to create a healthy, thriving organisation, but will also help attract and retain the best people to build the organisation's next brilliant phase.

Let's recap

We've now learnt how an organisation's degree of focus and its level of activity can impact on the wellbeing of its employees and influence outcomes for the organisation. To summarise:

WHEN THERE IS TOO MUCH HAPPENING WE:

» End up fighting the limited capacity of our brain and exacerbate this by trying to focus on too much at once

» Focus on short-term interests and work with a natural bias that inhibits sustainable work practices

» Allow our well intentioned drive to enable organisational multitasking that steals our success.

WHEN THERE IS TOO LITTLE HAPPENING WE:

» Lose confidence in our abilities as employees and can suffer physically and emotionally

» Have a lack of belief in the need to focus on maintaining a healthy culture, and a lack of ability to identify or implement what could help

» Inadvertently put the organisation in danger of failing.

WHEN WE START TO GET IT RIGHT WE:

» Identify and prioritise what matters

» Focus our attention on a single way to improve what we do and how we do it that supports our purpose

» Support the long-term health of our people and our organisation.

Whether we are working in an office or focusing in the field, doing knowledge work, service work or more physical labour, we need to pay close attention. Knowing *why* we are focused on *what* we are focusing on is what gives us the motivation to do our best.

PART 2
DOING IT DEEP

*Either you decide to stay in the shallow end
of the pool or you go out in the ocean.*[44]

CHRISTOPHER REEVE

Doing ONE THING requires action – the word 'doing' sort of gives it away. Identifying our ONE THING to do is a start, but how we do it also matters. We have seen organisations doing nothing and doing everything. Both options have poor outcomes for the wellbeing of people and the sustainability of businesses.

But even doing ONE THING comes in a few different flavours. And while we need this diversity of approaches, sometimes there is only one way to do it. Sometimes you need to do it deep.

So let's take a quick tour of the doing ONE THING world and then get a deeper understanding of deep.

CHAPTER 4
WAYS TO DO ONE THING

The shortest way to do many things
is to do only one thing at once.[45]

SAMUEL SMILES

ONE THINGs come in all shapes and sizes. They can be done for ourselves or to help others. They can be quick and easy, or difficult and time-consuming. They can be ways to prioritise or procrastinate. Let's look at a few examples.

Do ONE THING at a time

Earlier, we discussed how our attention is limited – we only have so much capacity to focus on activities. This is especially true of those activities that involve the brain's executive functions – focusing, planning, prioritising, decision making, emotional regulation, and initiating and persisting with tasks. We know that multitasking is actually task-switching,[46] which impacts how effective we are at getting stuff done.[47] So as a general rule, we can only focus on ONE THING, which is why doing ONE THING at a time works so well.

Do ONE THING now

When you're thinking about doing ONE THING now, it's often about getting something underway. To start your task or project, you need to do something immediately. One of my mentors instilled in me the benefits of not leaving a meeting with things still left to do – well, not things that can be taken care of before you walk out the door. Doing ONE THING now is a great way to be more efficient, build momentum and avoid the potential lure of procrastination.

Do ONE THING first

When you're thinking about doing ONE THING first, you're identifying priorities. Some things need to happen in order. To do the next thing, you may need to do ONE THING first. To be fair, it can also be a way to get out of something. Ever heard or said, 'I just have to do this ONE THING first. Then I can …'. (Yes, I see what you're up to there.)

Do ONE THING after another

While priorities put THINGs first, processes require that you do certain ONE THINGs sequentially. To achieve the THING, you need to follow the steps, like a recipe. Otherwise you could end up with a horse staring perplexed at a cart. I'm sure you've heard the expression, 'It's just ONE THING after another around here.' ONE THINGs are never-ending. There will always be issues that need addressing or areas that simply need more attention in any workplace. And that's just life, really.

Do ONE THING quickly

If you haven't asked this of yourself, I'm sure someone has said to you at some point, 'Could you just do this ONE THING quickly before you go?' This brings back to my mind the image of one of my bosses walking down the corridor in the late afternoon as I was about to leave work. As I was saying goodbye to people, these words would spring from her lips. Seeing as her many meetings had finished for the day, she looked to make a few more THINGs someone else's concern: mine! There is an implied 'more' in this expression, or an obligation. 'Could you just do this ONE THING quickly before you go?' translates as 'You have already been doing lots of things, but here is just another small, not very time consuming or difficult thing you could be doing. And, for some reason I won't explain, it's a priority for you to do it now.' My boss' last-minute ONE THINGs were rarely quick, rarely small, rarely ONE THING, and usually meant I was going nowhere. Time to put the handbag down.

Do ONE THING for someone

This request is related to the previous ONE THING we looked at, but fails to stress its character. 'There's ONE THING I need you to do for me' doesn't come with a caveat of 'quickly', or 'now', or 'first'. Let's face it, it could be any ONE THING. With this common way to ask for help, maybe check what it is before you say, 'Sure.'

Then there's the saying 'Do ONE THING every day that scares you' ... but I'm not going there. Too frightening.

Now that we've met a few possibilities for ONE THING-ing it, let's look more closely at doing ONE THING deep. I believe there are times when we're working on ourselves, in a team or for an organisation, when deep matters. I also believe we're often pretty bad at it, and that learning how to do ONE THING deep could just be the ONE THING we really need.

CHAPTER 5
THE PRINCIPLES OF DEEP

*Things which matter most must never be
at the mercy of things which matter least.*

JOHANN WOLFGANG VON GOETHE[48]

Deep means doing something well – being good at it. Mastering it, even. Shortly, we will talk about when deep is essential and when it's not. But for now, I'd like to share what deep means in the context of your ONE THING. I call these the Principles of Deep.

Do ONE THING that matters

Despite a residual and common misperception that people are rational economic actors doing just enough to satisfy their own self-interest, work has a greater importance to our identity. We want our work to be purposeful, to mean something, to make a difference in some way.

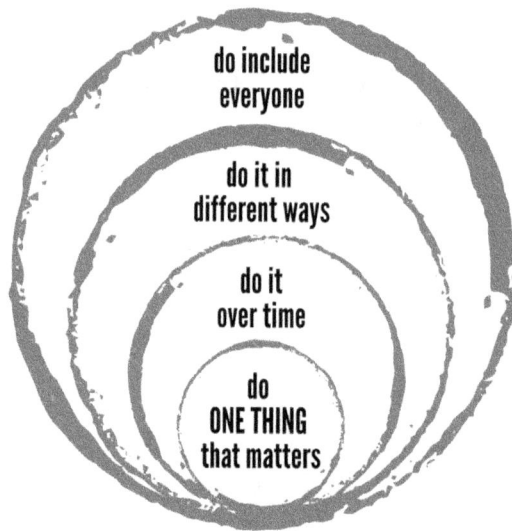

When you ask people to come on a ONE THING journey and go deep, you need to demonstrate that this ONE THING matters and it's something worth caring enough about to take action. Best-selling author and behaviour expert Dan Pink reminds us that we can't force people to do things. Still, we can move people by finding common ground, and one of the keys to doing that is to make it purposeful.[49]

When organisations rally behind an authentic higher purpose - an aspirational mission that explains how employees are making a difference and gives them a sense of meaning ... they will try new things, move into deep learning, and make surprising contributions. The workforce will become energized and committed, and performance will climb ... By tapping into that power, you can transform an entire organization.[50]

A recent report by the multinational professional services firm EY (Ernst & Young) states 'a sense of purpose should be at the center of a company's strategy for growth'.[51] Not only does it pay to have purpose, those with a strong capital-P Purpose build trust, connection and engagement. Having purpose enables companies to transform and innovate better. But the report also warns that it can't be window dressing. It must 'be driven, operationally and in depth, by the CEO and the top leadership team [and] ... go beyond an initiative that sits at the margins of the organization'. [52]

Making your ONE THING meaningful should align to your purpose and strategy – but it isn't always that lofty. Sometimes it will be a small action that is one requisite part of your larger purpose. Think of this smaller THING as one of the ribs of your ONE THING umbrella. It can be something very practical. In these instances, I find the phrase, 'And we will do that by ...' a helpful connector between the purpose and the ONE THING. For example, 'We will do our ONE THING deep by focusing on this area, starting with this action and doing it this way.' When you are working deep with your organisation's ONE THING, you might need to take one purposeful bite of your ONE THING apple at a time.

Do it over time

When you are invested in you and your organisation becoming good at its ONE THING, don't expect it to happen overnight. Whether you are learning something new yourself, working with a team to improve a process, skill or behaviour, or aiming to change your organisation's culture, it will take time.

It would be foolish to expect a positive shift in your workplace after hearing one rousing speech, attending a single workshop or reading one motivational poster. When I heard a leader say, 'I don't know why that's not happening ... I mentioned that at the town hall (communal workplace) meeting before last,' I was amazed at their expectations. In the same way, we can have unrealistic expectations of ourselves and others at times.

Say your organisation decides to focus on getting better at the ONE THING that's been decided on. Let's say it's the ONE THING that came up for you in your thought experiment. Not everyone will get on board as soon as it's announced. Like boarding an aeroplane, there will always be early and late boarders. You will need to offer more time for those who are cautious in adopting change. They need extra time to overcome their uncertainty by witnessing that it is safe. They need to see that the others who are doing this ONE THING are okay, recognise that there seem to be positive benefits to doing the ONE THING, and understand that there is support for doing it. Otherwise, people will get left behind and that will hold everyone back.

New and different takes time, patience and practice. So yes, deep needs time.

Do it in different ways

As well as taking the time to get on board and then become good at something, we need to acknowledge that not everyone learns or takes in information in the same way.[53] Any personality inventory can demonstrate a range of communication preferences. Some people relate better to models, statistics, case studies, stories, metaphors or images. So, if we are trying to reach every heart, mind and hand in the organisation, it seems wise to cover multiple bases.

In organisational culture change, this would mean ensuring a range of ways to encounter the same information. Different modes of information delivery could be employed, such as guest speakers, town halls, articles, marketing materials, training, etc. People need to regularly bump into the same message expressed in different ways.

It's like when you subtly suggest to a friend that they could make a small change in their behaviour, or take on a new activity they might like, or meet this person you think they might want to connect with, but they blindly ignore your sage advice. After a few attempts, you give up. Then months later, they come running up to you to share their new discovery. They've read a magazine or heard a podcast, or a different friend has mentioned this ONE THING that they realise will be really helpful and brilliant for them to do. All you can do is express how wonderful it is that they thought of it ... and hold back from saying you had already and repeatedly suggested this very thing.

And remember those people at the front of the queue to board the plane, the early adopters? They can get bored pretty easily.

So having novel ways to express the ONE THING will keep them engaged over time.

Do it with others

Work, learning and change are not journeys we take alone. We need to see how things fit together from multiple perspectives to solidly embed a new reality. Diverse opinions give us better options. And while it's not always a smooth ride, organisations that engage a diverse workforce, and encourage different ways of thinking and working, will achieve better results than those who do not. [54]

You need to be diligent about inclusion. Early engagement of the people this ONE THING will affect is critical. It's important to hear from and involve as many of those people as you can. As social psychologist and author Heidi Grant puts it, 'If you aren't actively including, you are probably accidentally excluding.'[55] However, some caution is required, as I have seen the fear of excluding people lead to over-inclusion.[56] This can burden your people unnecessarily.

The Principles of Deep acknowledge that things take time. Not everyone learns at the same pace. Deep recognises that people take up information and learn in different ways. Not everyone gets on board using the same tools. So to really make a difference, you need a few different approaches. To make a lasting impact, you need to involve as many of the right people as possible to allow a new normal or standard to emerge.

Deep matters when what you are doing matters. And if it doesn't matter, why are you doing it? Now that's deep.

Why deep matters

In organisations, things get done for many reasons (sometimes we might even know what they are). Maybe it's just to say a thing has been done and dusted. Or it was in the company's 30-year strategic plan. Or, from an individual perspective, it was one of your KPIs, or maybe all the other kids were doing it.

But deep is not a tick-the-box exercise. It's not quick and dirty. It's not about a one-and-done. It's not outsourcing responsibility. It's about harnessing our drive for building something meaningful that has a lasting impact.

We can apply the Principles of Deep to:

- organisations that are looking for lasting positive change

- teams that want to increase their performance

- individuals who are looking to master something new.

Deep is an engagement strategy. It attracts the right people and focuses your organisation. It's a way to build skills, generate trust and goodwill, and achieve things that make you proud. And that makes deep a great strategy for sustainability and resilience.

What happens when you ignore deep?

We have all experienced a lack of deep. Who hasn't done a workshop only to never use anything they learnt? Who hasn't had a project they've been working on shelved because of an inexplicable change in priorities? Who hasn't filled in a staff survey and never seen any tangible outcomes?

'Not deep' costs dollars. It's doing what's expedient, but it might not give a good return on investment. When turning that traffic light in the strategic plan from red to orange to green by this date is the primary goal, long-term efficacy can go out the window. This is especially true of an Every-THING workplace, with projects going off like popcorn in a microwave. 'Not deep' means we are setting ourselves up for failure.

Where we choose to focus our deep, extended and exclusive attention says a lot. It tells us what truly matters and even who we are. I think most workplaces want their employees to be proud of what they achieve. Most of us don't just work to say 'It's done' and then move on to the next thing, but because it's of service to our clients and makes a difference in some way. We want to align our purpose with that of the organisation.

Continually doing the quick fix is a waste of resources that erodes trust in a team or organisation. 'We tried this before, and it didn't work,' becomes more than someone whinging. Over time, it becomes a legitimate reason to think the next attempt will also be a waste of effort. When that new intervention, training or activity doesn't work, all subsequent similar attempts at change or improvement need to work that much harder. Once a change of any type is tarred with the brush of 'half-hearted', 'unengaging' or 'tick-the-box', it's hard to get the gunk out.

Is deep appropriate for everything?

It's true that if a thing's worth doing, it worth doing well. But some things aren't worth doing at all, and sometimes certain activities require only minimal effort. We can get tripped up on the need to do things 'properly' and that's not the same as doing them deep. In my mind, 'properly' is set by some external standard that might be wrong for the context, whereas deep is about lasting, meaningful results.

How do I know when I need to do something deep? Well, let's start here.

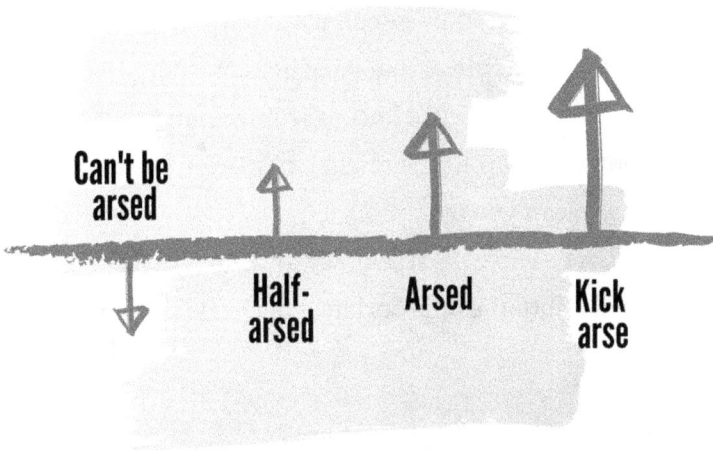

When I judge how much effort to put in for the outcome I want, I use the 'Arse Scale'. Now the Arse Scale isn't about doing a botched job. I am not looking to arse-it-up, just to apply the appropriate effort. This handy and slightly amusing scale has four levels.

Can't be arsed

This is the appropriate degree of effort for things that aren't worth doing at all. For example, attending a meeting that has nothing to do with your work and which you can't contribute to in any way. It's not essential and any time spent there is not going to have an impact. Perhaps it's a habit that isn't serving you any longer or something in the workplace culture that answers to, 'That's just how we've always done it around here.' Is it ineffective, purposeless or demoralising? Then stop wasting time on it.

Just check that the thing you can't be arsed about truly belongs in this category because it's not worth doing, rather than using 'can't be arsed' as a handy avoidance tactic. It's not an excuse for laziness, or to not do things that you should be doing. But if the task is just dull, complicated or time-consuming and still needs to be done by someone, perhaps it might not need to be done by you. If that's the case, can you outsource it?

And if it isn't a can't-be-arsed task and you are just being a bit of a sloth, move it into the appropriate Arse Scale category.

Half-arsed

Yes, you need to do this thing, but it doesn't need deep. It just needs to be done – just sort of, maybe, barely. This is the very valid half-arsed approach. It will not require all of your effort. Half-arsed means 'Near enough is good enough' trumps 'A thing worth doing is worth doing well.' This sort of task is not something you want to spend a lot of time on. For example, you don't need to read every single email first thing in the morning. It's enough to give them a look over and leave anything that's not critically important till later.

It's amazing how by leaving things for a little while, someone else who's responsible for it might have sorted it out. So a quick peruse and Bob's your uncle (whatever that means). Then you can turn your attention to more important things.

Arsed

Now we enter the category where you ask yourself, 'Can I be arsed?' and you answer, 'Yes, I had better be arsed about this.' This thing not only needs doing, but it also requires the result to be of a reasonably good standard. It's worth putting in the effort, taking a little more time. It requires some attention to detail. Going through those budget figures may not be your cup of tea, but if you want your organisation to have – and be able to spend – money in the new financial year, you'd better give it a good look over. It's important and getting it right or wrong will have an impact. So you better be arsed.

Kick arse

When you go full kick arse, you're thinking like this: This really matters to me, to the people I work with, and for the goals of the business. I am invested in the outcome. It is meaningful, will have a big impact, and therefore needs significant time and attention. I want this to shine, so I am ready, willing and able to go above and beyond.

If the term '110 per cent' didn't make me gag, doing your ONE THING to kick-arse level would be that – going full throttle, reaching above and beyond, doing it deep. Like showing my team they matter by not missing one-on-one meetings for anything less than the building catching on fire.

So as the Arse Scale shows, whatever we are working on, we choose our level of 'doing-ness'. By having a clear expectation about where things sit on this scale, you'll be less likely to arse around and waste time. Identifying the degree of effort required on the ONE THING you are doing means you can use your limited time and energy judiciously.

So when I know something needs my dedicated time and attention, even if it's not something I find fun, I think about how I can kick arse at doing it. And that means I need to do my ONE THING deep.

The road to deep

Are you up for a journey that focuses on what's important? One that is inclusive, incorporates diverse approaches and may take a little time? Well, you're in the right place.

The road to doing ONE THING deep will take some effort, but because it's about something that will make a difference, it will be worth it. Using the Principles of Deep will help your organisation achieve meaningful outcomes.

With a clear idea of a ONE THING and an understanding of the benefits of doing it deep, the next step for you, your leadership team and your organisation is to start on your *do*-ONE THING-*deep* journey.

Let's recap

» Go deep on your ONE THING. That is, find something meaningful to work on, do it over time, in different ways and involve others.

» Do your THING any way you choose, but ask the question, 'Does this need deep?' Not everything does.

» Don't skimp on a THING that requires your full and deep attention, as it can end up costing you time, money, and the goodwill and trust of your people.

So what's the next step? It's time to take action.

PART 3
NOW YOU DO IT

*Attention is key; for where a man's attention goes,
there his energy goes, and he himself can only follow.*[57]

COUNT OF ST GERMAIN

Now doing ONE THING deep is great in theory, but let's get into what you actually need to do. If you are a leader in an organisation that wants to make change happen, especially to its culture, it's time to take your first steps into *doing*-ONE THING-*deep* territory. This includes choosing your ONE THING and developing a *do*-ONE THING-*deep* campaign. Getting these early steps right is important if your organisation is to realise and work with the Principles of Deep – knowing what matters, doing it over time and in different ways, and being inclusive. But there are also traps to avoid and things that can speed your journey when you do this. So to help you and your organisation on your *do*-ONE THING-*deep* journey, let's look at some traveller's notes on the terrain.

CHAPTER 6
THE DO-ONE THING-
DEEP JOURNEY

If everyone is moving forward together,
then success will take care of itself.[58]

HENRY FORD

Wouldn't it be great if this section could outline a simple three-step ONE THING solution that will guarantee success in only seven days or your money back? But who are we kidding? This is not any old THING. A *do*-ONE THING-*deep* journey is about people deciding what matters, engaging in identifying what's needed to do that brilliantly and getting it done.

An integral part of any *do*-ONE THING-*deep* journey is choosing an appropriate and useful ONE THING to work on. Identifying your organisation's ONE THING won't be the same as the British Rowing Eight asking, 'Will it make the boat go faster?' But, just as they did, you *will* focus on your organisation's ONE THING from every possible perspective, engaging everyone over time to achieve success.

Let's delve into some principles and practices that can help with choosing your ONE THING and mapping your *do*-ONE THING-*deep* journey. Think of these as tools for harnessing your organisation's energy to help align the why, what and how of your company. Remember, a great ONE THING done deep will re-energise your people, produce outstanding outcomes and create a vibrant and motivated workplace.

Why culture matters

There is a growing realisation of the importance of a positive work culture to our businesses and services[59] because it's what 'makes the boat go faster'. It's no longer simply something that's nice to have. Mature organisations take working on their culture as seriously as any service or product.[60] We have seen numerous examples where serious issues have arisen because a poor culture was ignored and became toxic.[61] And it's not hard to recall recent scandals that have led to investigations or royal commissions.

Organisational culture is more than the perks and environment of a company.[62] It's not all about ping-pong tables, beanbags and a barista. Organisational culture is variously described as 'The way we do things around here' or 'What happens when the manager leaves the room.'[63] It's a vibe thing.

An article in Forbes magazine describes culture rather well:

Typically, corporate culture is what energizes us or drains us, it motivates us or discourages us, it empowers us or it suffocates us. We all experience the corporate culture of our organizations every single day, whether it be positive or negative.[64]

Research tells us that a great culture increases employee happiness, client satisfaction, productivity and profitability.[65] But you don't work directly on culture. A great organisational culture is the by-product of working on everything that makes your business great for your people and your customers. Transforming a poor corporate culture to an outstanding one starts with an organisation working on ONE THING – and working on it together. Fostering a good corporate culture relies on senior leadership being responsible for setting the tone.[66] Leaders need to focus their team and guide their attention to working together on common goals. They need to lead their people by identifying the organisation's ONE THING and supporting them in realising their ONE THING goal.

Culture change isn't easy

Positively shifting the dial on culture can be difficult. A common and widely accepted statistic tells us that 70 per cent of change initiatives fail[67] due to employee resistance and lack of management support (although it's also suggested that this percentage may be an overestimation[68]). Speaking personally, many of the attempts at improving corporate culture I have experienced haven't been great. They failed to achieve what they set out to do and demoralised employees to boot.

Why does attempting to change an organisation's culture fail? The complexity of cultural change can see leaders not wanting to step into the arena or they view it as strictly an HR issue.[69] Alternatively, in an enthusiastic burst, they might launch multiple initiatives at once in the hope of fixing things quickly,[70] with the result that nothing gets fixed at all.

While fostering a good corporate culture is part of every employee's role, it is the single most critical focus for the CEO and a significant aspect of any leader's or leadership team's responsibility.[71] And when there are so many matters jostling for attention, it takes courage for a leader to concentrate on ONE THING, yet doing so is vital. Engaging everyone through different methods over time on ONE THING will have a positive, lasting impact and create a ripple effect that builds trust, connection and engagement across the organisation, both for the business itself and for its people.

So choosing ONE THING to focus on can channel energy into something positive. Even the energy of uncertainty, frustration and ennui can be transformed. People working together on something tangible, something that matters to the outcomes for the organisation and improves the experience of working there, will create a renewed sense of purpose. This will build the business, foster and support strength, and increase engagement. And that's a great culture.

CHAPTER 7
GETTING ONE THING WRONG

Learn from the mistakes of others. You can't live
longe enough to make them all yourself.[72]

ELEANOR ROOSEVELT

🚫

Some of the barriers to working on strengthening the culture in an organisation are specific to a No-THING and Every-THING workplace.

As we have seen in Part 1 of this book, in an Every-THING workplace there can be an addiction to activity – there's always something happening. It can appear as if a form of short-termism akin to organisational Attention Deficit Disorder[73] has taken hold.

There is an inability to prioritise and say no, and increasingly self-interested silos are formed.

In a No-THING workplace, where nothing ever happens, there is an underlying aversion to risk that can create a suspicion around the value of working on cultural change. The difficulty in making a decision and saying yes to anything means there is little hope of implementing change effectively.

Aside from these two distinct (at times equally frustrating) workplace styles, there are some other things to look out for that can get in the way of improving the cultural wellbeing of an organisation. Let's take a look at some common ways that attempts at organisational change can go pear-shaped.

People are not included or engaged in decision making

People want to feel heard. They want to have the things that matter to them taken seriously,[74] even when they are small things. Without this, any organisational initiative is vulnerable to inertia or, worse still, active undermining by the very people it's intended to benefit.

To support positive change, it's best not to start down this road by *telling* people what they should be doing. Instead, *ask* them, early and often, how the proposed change – how the ONE THING the organisation needs to focus on – could work. In discovering and creating your ONE THING, deliberate engagement is vital. Employees being actively involved in decision making and seeing ONE THING carried through to completion builds trust – not with everyone immediately, but over less time than you might think.

Poor sponsorship

It would be hard to overstate how critical it is to have full support from leaders for an organisation's ONE THING. In fact, I won't try, so brace for bluntness. If your ONE THING isn't taken seriously by each member of the senior leadership team, it won't be effective. If this is left for HR and Comms to do with a half-arsed steering committee, don't bother. You will do less damage by NOT doing ONE THING. Spend the money on a picnic instead, which will at least be a fun afternoon.

I would love to say that there is a way for a frontline groundswell of interest and action to autonomously achieve ONE THING. But without unified and high-level support, gains are easily destroyed by egos and politics. In the next section, we will delve deeper into how your organisation's leaders can step fully into the role of being ONE THING sponsors. For now, these three points are key to the kind of sponsorship that will drive your ONE THING's success.

Leaders need to:

- actively stay across what's happening with your ONE THING, keep it front-of-mind to identify opportunities for deepening understanding and engagement, and maintain the energy around the ONE THING

- visibly and consistently live up to the standards and behaviours that align with the ONE THING and hold to account those who don't

- share a clear, consistent message until it feels like overcommunicating (it's not).

Declaring 'mission accomplished' too soon

Quite often, organisations do not allow enough time for initiatives to really make a lasting impact. A great deal of effort goes into the initial activity – the big announcement, the reveal, the launch event. The nitty-gritty implementation is not as fun and shiny. To succeed, the effort must be sustained.

Remember deep? Some people will embrace your ONE THING immediately and enthusiastically. Others will be wary or cynical, especially if they have seen new ideas or attempts at change fail in the past. Failures with previous initiatives tend to stick in the organisational memory for a long time. I recall an employee in one organisation explaining to me why a particular initiative would not work. This is a healthy discussion to have. Still, in this instance, the rationale for the impending failure was because something similar had been tried and done very badly twelve years ago. That was eight years before the employee had started with the company.

People need to hear a message many times, in many ways, often, frequently and, dare I say, repeatedly, before some of them become advocates. So don't call 'Time' too early.

We live in a world where the long term is not a priority. Short term is even a part of how our brains work. We would rather have one marshmallow now than wait for two in a little while – even if we know that two is better. But taking ONE THING slowly and sinking both marshmallows deep into the hot chocolate of our organisational psyche will ultimately be worthwhile. Oh, dear … I think that analogy got away from me.

CHAPTER 8
GETTING ONE THING RIGHT

Outstanding people have one thing in common:
an absolute sense of mission.[75]

ZIG ZIGLAR

What if you could find ONE THING you wanted to bake into the culture of your organisation? Something that could address your most pressing concerns or accelerate a significant achievement? One cultural focal point that you and your people will spend several months to a year working through to make it brilliant?

You've found it? Okay, you're set. But someone is bound to ask, 'Who has time for that?' Maybe a better question, though, would be: 'Who has the time and resources to waste on doing nothing, doing everything or doing the wrong thing and disengaging or overwhelming your people?'

Make the time and use it wisely by engaging your workforce and considering the different ways people learn and respond to new ideas. Remember that some will embrace a new shared ONE THING quickly, while others need more time and effort to see the value of adopting this ONE THING and doing it every day.

Embracing the power of attention in your organisation, creating a sense of possibility around this ONE THING, and inviting everybody to work on it together will have a profound impact. And remember, the beauty of focusing on ONE THING is that it:

- won't overwhelm people in an already busy workplace
- clarifies what matters and creates a greater sense of satisfaction
- is more sustainable and effective.

What if you could identify, implement and evaluate ONE THING, deploy it over time in different ways, and include your people in creating deep, meaningful value? Well you'll see some magic start to happen.

Find your ONE THING

Finding the right ONE THING can be a bit of a dark art, but there are many ways to get there. The quest starts with data from your organisation's purpose, mission, values and strategy. If you have these handy, along with the most recent staff survey, you are already on your way to finding some prospective ONE THINGs. Or you can start by simply asking your people. Remember the exercise we did at the beginning of this book, where I asked you to think about some things you believe your organisation could do better? I bet you came up with a few ideas quite easily. There isn't a lack of ideas out there, it's finding and shaping the right one that is tricky. But it's entirely achievable.

Here is another way to ask that question. It comes from Gary Keller's Wall Street Journal bestseller, The One Thing:[76] The surprisingly simple truth behind extraordinary results.[77] He has what he calls his focusing question. I find this remarkably helpful for finding a ONE THING to do deep. Gary asks, 'What's the one thing I/we can do such that by doing it, everything else will be easier or unnecessary?'

But as well as accelerating efficency, your ONE THING will:

- align with your purpose and values, which is the key for engagement
- resonate, or have the potential to resonate, with a broad range of people
- have some built-in flexibility, meaning it's narrow enough to be contained but also offers room for some variation in how it's used.

Check these ideas out with your people – from senior leadership to frontline – as you explore your ONE THING options and decide on what to do. Even if it's not the single most crucial, best-ever ONE THING you could do, the success of that ONE THING – chosen for the organisation and by the organisation – can positively affect your workplace's culture. It tells people that they can make change happen.

Sleuth your ONE THING

Keep in mind that baking-in your organisational ONE THING doesn't mean randomly doing a few things like putting up a poster and buying some new lanyards. You'll need to explore what it really means by sleuthing out the **beliefs** of your organisation and its people, the **structures** that will support this ONE THING, and the **agency** of all involved – including yours. Answering a few questions about these can help you understand the nature of the particular ONE THING you and your people will be working on. Questions like these.

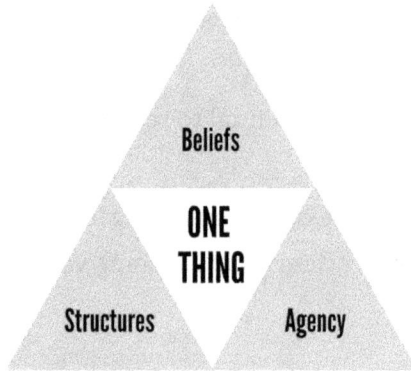

Beliefs

It's crucial to identify beliefs that support or inhibit success. What are the current beliefs about your ONE THING, both in the organisation in general, and in the leadership team in particular? What values are actively demonstrated? What's outlined around this in your workplace's key organisational documents? What informal stories are told?

Structures

Your ONE THING lives in the bones of your organisation. Where and how is your ONE THING represented in your policies and processes, your physical environment and infrastructure, your organisational structure, across the employee lifecycle and in communications? Where can these supporting structures be helpful to your ONE THING's success and where do they act to stymie good practice? If your ONE THING doesn't fit into existing structures, can you adapt those structures or create new ones?

Agency

Once people believe the ONE THING is valuable, they need useful and meaningful ways to apply it in activities that align with what they do. How do people currently engage with your ONE THING? Is that interaction easy for them? Do they have a degree of autonomy? Do they have the right capabilities and enough capacity? What aspects of this ONE THING do people have ownership of?

Start your ONE THING

So now you have an idea of what baking-in your ONE THING entails and it's time to start your ONE THING. Here are a few key ingredients to remember:

- Spend some time identifying the right ONE THING, but don't get stuck there

- Immerse your people in the decision-making process and in the project itself: a sense of meaningful involvement bolsters engagement

- Overcommunicate over time: leaders should keep repeating the message in different ways and through various channels. (Yes, I just keep coming back to that one.)

Above all, make space for creativity and fun. Don't confuse doing change-inducing work with a need to be serious. Working on your ONE THING together with your organisation doesn't need to be dull.

Let's recap

» When you are starting out on your *do*-ONE THING-*deep* journey, there will be potholes and road bumps that will get in your way. And there will be smooth straight freeways that speed you along. But getting the workplace culture right is a journey worth taking, With the evidence for toxic cultures so visible, mature organisations treat building a great one as seriously as any product or service.

» ONE THINGs go wrong when people are not engaged, there is poor sponsorship, or organisations throw in the towel too early.

» Finding your ONE THING to do deep and digging deeply into the beliefs, structures and agency that hold you back will speed you towards a healthy and productive organisational culture.

Now that you're committed to embarking on a *do*-ONE THING-*deep* journey, let's look at what makes a great *do*-ONE THING-*deep* campaign.

PART 4
THREE CAMPAIGNS AND ONE THING

Attention is the rarest and purest form of generosity.[78]

SIMONE WEIL

Now that you and your organisation know what your ONE THING is, it's time to make it happen by creating a do-ONE THING-deep campaign. There are several types of successful ONE THING campaigns. They can be big and loud – with carnivalesque launch events, high-profile speakers and lots of investment in wall-to-wall branding. Or they can be small and subtle – with good two-way information sharing and leaders personally engaging with teams and individuals. Each ONE THING campaign will be different because of the organisational context, and each will depend on the singular vision and strategic priorities of the organisation. Regardless of its style, any good do-ONE THING-deep campaign should reflect key aspects of the business, such as the industry, the organisation's core values, and the level of maturity and growth.

Political Campaign

Engagement Campaign

Marketing Campaign

There are also valuable lessons to learn about conducting your do-ONE THING-deep campaign by looking at different campaign disciplines. Like speaking different languages, they can bring a richer, deeper perspective to your journey. In this section, we'll look at three types of campaign in detail, each of which will play a part in your organisation's ONE THING campaign.

- The first is the political campaign. This is not about any preconceived notions of partisan politics, but about leadership.

- The second is the engagement campaign. This campaign has a social, community or employee-engagement focus. It's about making sure you and your organisation get people on board and use their particular gifts and contributions as much as possible.

- The third is the marketing campaign. The Principles of Deep talk about how you and your organisation need to use different ways to send out a clear and engaging message – and this is how to do it.

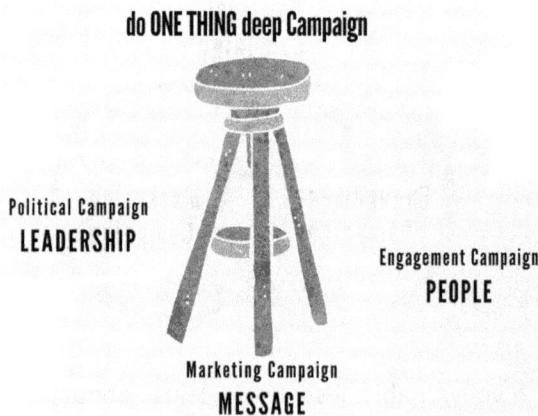

do ONE THING deep Campaign

Political Campaign
LEADERSHIP

Engagement Campaign
PEOPLE

Marketing Campaign
MESSAGE

These three campaigns are like a three-legged stool. If you don't have the legs even or equal, your ONE THING campaign will not be stable. Or at the very least, it will be a little wobbly and let's face it, no one wants that.

If your leadership team isn't supporting the message and actively engaging people, it won't seem important enough for anyone to participate. This is especially true if your leaders do not demonstrate the behaviours or actions that your ONE THING requires.

If your people aren't involved, don't feel heard or don't have an opportunity to share their perspectives, it can seem like this ONE THING is being imposed from above. Without the proper engagement needed for success, your do-ONE THING-deep campaign will be much less effective.

If the message isn't right, your leaders and your people won't engage. It must be meaningful and in tune with the organisation. No one likes a tone-deaf message or one that's irrelevant. They all work together – the leaders, the people and the message.

Now saddle up partners, it's time to hit the campaign trail. As you and your organisation travel along your ONE THING journey, you can track each of your do-ONE THING-deep campaign's key elements through a scenic campaign trail. Here are the not-to-miss sights you'll need to visit:

- **Commit** – There are many ways to support your organisation's development, but first you have to decide that you will do this ONE THING. Make the commitment. Are you in – like, *all in* – or are you out?

The CAMPAIGN Trail

COMMIT
You don't know what your ONE THING is yet, but you are committed to finding out and following through.

LISTEN
Build awareness by seeking to understand the needs and expectations of the group.

SAY
Identify your ONE THING and establish the key messages and ideas.

DO
Make it clear what is going to happen and what the expectations are for all concerned.

PLAY
Get everyone involved over time, in different ways and keep it fresh.

DESTINATION
Your ONE THING is established and continuing to evolve.

- **Listen** – Now give your people a good listening to. Hear their concerns. Find out what excites them and what they think this ONE THING could be or how it could work.

- **Say** – Decide on your ONE THING and why it matters. You need to be very clear about the message.

- **Do** – Now it's about doing. Does everyone understand the course of action, what it means for how you'll all work together, and your responsibilities to yourselves and others?

- **Play** – And now, you play the game. Be focused on getting everyone involved, keep the momentum and sustain engagement throughout the journey. And don't forget to have fun!

- **Destination** – With persistence, consistent engagement over time and reviewing your progress, you have reached your ONE THING destination. Ready to start again?

CHAPTER 9
THE POLITICAL CAMPAIGN

Leaders concentrate single-mindedly on ONE THING – the most important thing, and they stay at it until it's complete.[79]

BRIAN TRACY

Let's just deal with this upfront. Aligning the idea of *do*-ONE THING-*deep* with a political campaign can really put people off. Watching the current state of politics in some places and learning about corrupt actors from the media cause deep distrust of those in office and the system itself. To be clear, the focus here isn't on party politics. It's not about campaigns that go negative and concentrate on discrediting others. Or, for that matter, on disseminating vicious attack ads, boring us with bland statements or obvious duplicity and saying anything to get elected.

Our focus in this chapter is primarily on learning from those who run great campaigns to help get leaders elected. Leaders who concentrate on issues they care about, who genuinely want to serve the public and who want to get stuff done. Exploring what we can learn from these professional campaigners and committed leaders will help us think about how we too could lead and engage others through a strong do-ONE THING-deep campaign.

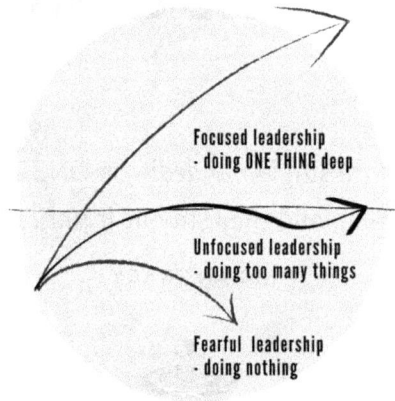

Focused leadership
- doing ONE THING deep

Unfocused leadership
- doing too many things

Fearful leadership
- doing nothing

Remember, having your leadership team sponsor your ONE THING campaign is critical to success. So let's map out the political campaign for a ONE THING. Join me on this journey – because if you see the value of helping your people and organisation to focus on a do-ONE THING-deep campaign, you better know what you are up for.

Leadership

COMMIT
Decide to run.

LISTEN
Take a listening tour.

SAY
Master the message.

DO
Accountability matters.

PLAY
Play your ground game.

DESTINATION
Celebrate and reflect.

Decide to run

In a political campaign, the first thing someone needs to do is decide to run as a candidate for ONE THING. As a leader, you choose to take on the role of sponsor. It's not a decision to take lightly. Being unfocused and not committed to the journey will negatively affect the success of your organisational ONE THING.

The question that every politician needs to be able to answer is, 'Why are you running?' As a leader, you need to know this for yourself before you decide. If *you* don't buy into the *do*-ONE THING-*deep* campaign ethos, neither will anyone else and you will waste time and resources, as well as the goodwill of your constituents.

Before you fully commit, know what the role entails. Walk the rest of the journey's route to understand what's ahead and to know what playing full out looks like. Deciding to run shows that you are a solid citizen and dedicated to the wellbeing of the organisation (or the country).

Keep in mind that leading a ONE THING campaign is an excellent opportunity to deepen your leadership capabilities, gain new experiences and connect more broadly across the organisation. As well as potentially being a smart career move, a well designed and implemented *do*-ONE THING-*deep* campaign is the best leadership development program you can do.

Take a listening tour

You may have noticed that in the lead up to a campaign, politicians often set out on a listening tour. Yes, it's all coming back to you now, isn't it? The big bus sets off (okay, sometimes around marginal seats) to hear what the constituents have to say. This is different from the actual campaign because the messages on a listening tour flow from the populace to the candidate, not the other way around. It's an opportunity to get an understanding of what's on the minds of the people. And it's best to do this listening tour before your ONE THING is really locked down.

In old-fashioned business-speak, this is called 'management by walking around.'[80] It was a popular theory in the 1970s and 80s. Bosses in hierarchical workplaces would make an effort to get out of their offices and talk to their employees. Some places did this really well. The boss was just someone you saw in the workplace who was genuinely interested in what you did and what you thought. It was no big deal. In other places, leaders would schedule fifteen minutes here or there, depending on where the successes or 'issues' were. News that the head honcho was about to 'do that thing where they walk around' would filter through to the relevant area, and there would be flurry of tidying up in evidence or mass disappearances.

In a ONE THING scenario, your listening tour will include opportunistic encounters: checking in with your direct reports, talking to people in kitchens, chatting to co-workers while waiting for the lift. But these chats can be planned. Courageous ONE THING leaders may even seek out people who are known to have different opinions in order to engage them as well.

Whichever way they are done, these encounters could be as simple as saying '(insert greeting and genuine interest about the person and what they do, etc.)' followed by:

- 'Hey, what do you think about how we do (insert potential ONE THING) here?'

- 'The leadership team is talking about working on (ONE THING) as an organisation. Would that help your team or the people you deal with here?'

- 'What would make how we do (ONE THING) better? Do you have any advice on how we could improve?'

- 'I am talking to a few people about how we do (ONE THING). I'd love to hear your thoughts. And do you know someone else that might have strong opinions on this I could talk to?'

- 'If you had a magic wand and we could work on any ONE THING as an organisation, what do you think would have the biggest impact?'

While it might take a bit more organising with a remote workforce, in general, this approach is not difficult. It doesn't need to be overly time-consuming, and it's not another darn survey.

Master the message

One significant aspect of your role in creating a successful *do*-ONE THING-*deep* campaign is to provide clarity.[81] The impact from a great campaign message is immeasurable (except to the boffins who make a living out of measuring that sort of thing). Remember 'It's time' or 'Yes we can' or 'Make America great again'? A single statement that adeptly crystalises what is to be achieved will be compelling. And once your organisational ONE THING has been identified, it's up to you to be across it and stay on message. Find out what support is available to keep you up to date and ask for what else you might need.

You'll also need to do some prep work.

What does 'staying on message' mean? Well, it's not that deflection thing some politicians do on the campaign trail. For example, a reporter asks, 'How's your dog?'

The candidate replies, 'Well, I'm glad you asked me about tax reform.'

No, we are going for a bit more authenticity than that.

You will need to understand your ONE THING information, know what's currently happening with it and be across the agreed way to share that information. When leadership team members give wildly different messages, it can be confusing and undermine the impact you hope to make.

I know I have said this before, but repetition is vital. (See what I did there?) Think about sharing the message and sharing it often, like a ONE THING stump speech. Political candidates will head out onto the hustings and give the same speech hundreds of times. They get very bored with it, but each new audience is hearing it for the first time. Plus, there will be contextual tweaks along the way to make it relevant to different constituencies. Our Principles of Deep tell us that we need to give people time to understand this new idea and put it out there in different ways. You will need to keep it fresh, perhaps adjust it for context, but the most important thing is to keep saying it.

The good news is that you are talking about an issue that really matters to you and your voters ... err ... I mean employees. And you know this can make a difference. So it's no colossal burden.

Accountability matters

It's not just what you say. Do-ONE THING-*deep* campaign sponsors, like political campaigners, need to be hyper-aware of their actions and the actions of those around them. The 24/7 news cycle will highlight where politicians' words and actions come unglued in a campaign. As a leader, everything you do is under scrutiny. People are watching all your actions, decisions, behaviours, who you are and are not talking to, what you have for lunch ... it's a bit creepy, really. So, make sure that whatever you say aligns with what you do. They must be the same.

What would living your ONE THING look like? And what expectations do you have for your leadership team and your employees to do the same? Once you know what they are, spend a little time reflecting on how you have fared with your ONE THING in the past. We've all seen politicians spruiking something in a campaign and being caught out by not having walked the talk previously. This will have a detrimental impact on their message. So how will you show up and model the behaviours, or engage in the activities, that go hand in hand with your ONE THING?

Doing what's required of a ONE THING leader means doing it consistently. Being a bit obvious at times also doesn't hurt. Leadership coach and author Marshall Goldsmith talks about doing the right thing and being seen to do it.[82] In one example, Goldsmith's right thing is to stop saying 'but' or 'however' when talking with his team. 'I like your idea but …' falls into this category. To him, it means, 'I am about to totally disagree with everything you just said before these words.' It demoralises people and stops them from speaking up.

His solution to this was to ask his team to fine him $20 whenever he uttered those words. Putting your money where your mouth is can be an excellent incentive for behaviour change. Goldsmith found out just how helpful his team were willing to be, and how deep and unconscious this habit was for him. After only an hour or so, he locked himself in his office with a considerably lighter wallet.[83] Goldsmith's solution might not be exactly right for your situation but you get the idea. Be prepared to walk your talk and put your hand up when you get it wrong. You build a deeper level of trust with people if you acknowledge where you too are still a work-in-progress with your ONE THING. Seeking help from others to hold you to account is a big plus. Being a bit vulnerable demonstrates to your people that everyone in the organisation is learning to do this together.

Being a little obvious about changing your behaviours can sound contrived, a trick, artificial. But it doesn't have to be. You may need to check you have un-ego-ed your approach, though. You are not trying to say, 'Look at me, I'm getting great at this.' Instead, you're going for the more subtle, 'This is important and I'm on board.'

Consistent modelling matters. It gives you the authority to do another important thing that ONE THING leaders need to do, and that's to hold others to account. This doesn't mean that you are punishing wrongdoers and need a bodysuit, cape and crazy secret identity. Being an Avenger should be a last resort – although one you are prepared for if necessary.

Think of yourself less as a comic book hero and more like a very talented first responder. What support can you offer? The aim is for everyone to work together towards this ONE THING goal. This will look different to different people. Some people take more time than others. Some resist in the first instance because they have had a bad ONE THING experience. Rather than telling people off for non-compliance, try helping first. Be curious to understand their response and offer support.

On the flip side, recognise and reward great ONE THING-ness in others. This is a subtle art. Not everyone wants 76 trombones and a big parade. Often, a quiet acknowledgement or a personal letter is all that's needed. A great ONE THING leader will have a variety of ways to recognise excellence and will make the effort to discover what's appropriate for each situation or person. Perhaps you can encourage those who are great at this ONE THING to support those who are struggling.

So in summary: be the change you want to see, listen to those with differing ideas and support them to find their way. Hold those who would undermine the benefits of this ONE THING to account and reward excellence in others. Embracing accountability is key to a smooth do-ONE THING-deep campaign.

Play your ground game

So you've made the decision to run as the leader. You know your role. You live the ONE THING message and you have a deep conviction about how this will benefit others. But no leader does this alone. You are going to need help beyond your campaign team.

Your job now is to garner support or 'activate your ground game'. You may know it as the grip and grin, kissing babies, smiling through endless townhall meetings, and wrists that need strapping after all that handshaking. It never seems to end. Unlike your listening tour, this is about getting the message out and people doing this ONE THING better. A ONE THING leader doesn't waste any opportunity to build and sustain the momentum in their campaign.

Luckily you don't need to phone people for financial donations. Still, you do need to find advocates who are willing to support the work. These people will mobilise action on your behalf. For a politician, this means having people in the community who will help. They will promote you, run bake sales and get others to the polling station to make a mark on a ballot on that one special day. Your job is to encourage people to encourage *more* people to take action around your ONE THING.

This is where the rubber hits the road on your *do*-ONE THING-*deep* campaign journey. It's every day for many, many days and weeks, and sometimes months. There are both uphill and downhill paths along the way. Being a ONE THING leader on the campaign trail is a test of endurance. But when the dopamine kicks in, something magical happens. You start to see positive changes and get to support others through challenges. You watch as people's thinking shifts, and you see their 'Aha' moment. When this happens, walking the campaign trail becomes no effort at all. Instead, it nourishes you.

Celebrate and reflect

For a ONE THING leader, the reward is what you learn along the journey about yourself, your people and the organisation. It's noticing the positive changes that occur as the goals of your ONE THING are achieved. It's the incidentals of deepening trust and creating a psychologically safer environment for learning and connection.

At the end of the ONE THING campaign, the leader must take the time to recognise and celebrate achievements. At this point, it's not unusual to feel the magnetic pull of doing the next ONE THING – because there are always and invariably more ONE THINGs to do. And you should. But first, you must show people the gains – the tangible and intangible, the small and personal, all the significant team and organisational achievements.

This is the time to stop and celebrate.

You need to close the loop between the goal and the achievement and clearly show this to your people. This will keep everyone motivated to improve and eager to join you on the next *do*-ONE THING-*deep* journey.

Now is also the moment to consider how your ONE THING could have gone better. What else could you have done and what have you learnt? Encourage the sharing of lessons with your team and celebrate that learning.

More personally, it's also a time to reflect on how this journey has made you a better leader, and the road you still have to travel to be the leader you aspire to be. Think about how you will continue to do the everyday, challenging and joyous work that is essential to being a great leader.

If we take a moment to backtrack around the trail, we can see how the Principles of Deep come to the fore during this process. There is focus on ONE THING that matters. ONE THING leaders listen to and engage as many people as they can. They give people time to come to an understanding of the ONE THING by repeating the message. And they contextualise it for different circumstances and employees.

This approach isn't something additional that leaders do. It's something that is woven into the fabric of their role and their workday. Think of it as a lens to view leadership through, rather than another set of tasks to add to the list. What you see through this lens provides you with an opportunity to understand the organisation and appreciate the different human beings who inhabit it with you. It helps leaders understand themselves, their organisations and to grow in their role.

CHAPTER 10
THE ENGAGEMENT CAMPAIGN

*There is no power for change greater than
a community discovering what it cares about.*[84]

MARGARET J WHEATLEY

Engagement campaigns come in many forms. They can work with specific groups – employees, a community, citizens and customers – and focus on any number of outcomes. But if they are worth their salt, they use the perspective, experience and strengths of the group to drive purposeful and needed change.

It used to be that the boss was the boss, and they told you what to do. But let's face it, that was a while ago now. The 2020 Edelman

Trust Survey found that 73 per cent of employees expect to be included in planning.[85] Clearly, there is a high expectation among employees of being heard. We know robust engagement with those affected improves the outcomes of the campaign. It can also be more complex, expensive and time-consuming than unilateral decision making, although that might only be true if you are using short-term measures. Maybe we need to find new and better ways and simply get good at engagement.

The evidence for engagement

Organisations obsess about employee engagement but don't always practice great engagment in the process. Surveys are conducted, but participation is low. Results are shared, but interpretation is unsupported, slipshod or mishandled. And the commitment and capability to take action is marred by individual and structural challenges.[86]

In change initiatives, research done by Gartner Inc. demonstrates how 'open source' methodology, which engages those affected early, is more effective than the more traditional top-down approach.[87]

The same is true with community engagement carried out by organisations and government bodies. Nothing erodes trust and goodwill faster than lack of consultation and projects that don't target real needs. Even high-profile and well-resourced projects can fail when people feel that something is being done to them and not with them.[88] Governments are being warned that failure to move to a partnership approach will see services become increasingly ineffective.[89]

But forget project success for a moment. Think about the people. Community engagement doesn't just improve services or increase their use. Non-participation has been shown to create a sense of powerlessness that negatively impacts individuals and the community's health and wellbeing.[90]

Wicked problems and diverse voices

Many of the issues we face in organisations today can be characterised as unrelenting, complex and likely to create unintended consequences – in short, wickedly difficult. They need 'savvy humans to collaborate and find solutions'.[91] So organisations are finding new ways to engage. They are moving beyond checking the box in a survey and onto more inclusive and democratic processes, such as citizen juries[92] and deliberative engagement.[93]

Where there is group diversity, there is a significant improvement in decision making,[94] employee engagement and trust,[95] leading to higher business returns.[96] It's increasingly evident that encouraging a range of voices with different skills, experience, ages, genders and cultures to consider issues, make decisions, create and initiate action is critical to success.

Check-the-box consultation

Of course, there are still organisations where 'consultation' remains a check-the-box exercise. The question becomes, 'What's the least I can do to say I consulted on this?' There *are* reasons to go it alone with initiatives, but not all of them are good.

Let's acknowledge that seeking engagement is not an easy route to take. Harnessing diverse skills, interests, capability, ideas, opinions and approaches is not without friction. While a little friction is good, we know it's not always comfortable.

When people are engaged in identifying, planning and decision making early in an initiative, it takes a little more time to get the project started. Organisations are often keen to get moving and deliver results, both good things in themselves, but paying a small upfront engagement fee by involving your people saves unexpected costs at the other end of the project. You discover issues you hadn't thought of, impacts on people and processes you hadn't anticipated, and even better and less costly solutions. Plus, getting people engaged early on will ease the path of your ONE THING implementation.

Take the following example. In a recent downturn, a respected architectural firm – let's call it ABC & Co – brought everyone together to discuss the implications for the firm and its immediate viability. They didn't keep the doors to the C-suite closed. Leaders were frank about the situation and about their hopes to keep everyone employed because each and every member of the business mattered. In discussions over a couple of weeks, employees came up with some remarkable suggestions to lower costs. These included adjustments to wages, reorganisation of working hours, finding better providers or eliminating some services, and honing procurement. This didn't just mean that they made it through a very tough time, but the firm's level of engagement built and maintained a greater sense of trust and connection.

People

COMMIT
Decide the approach.

LISTEN
Get your people on board.

SAY
Align activities.

DO
Manage the team.

PLAY
Take action.

DESTINATION
Fully engaged ONE THING.

If engagement truly matters to you (and if it doesn't, why are you doing it?), take the time to engage deeply with your people. Account for the additional upfront time it could take and nurture the different approaches that will help smooth the path for your ONE THING initiative.

So are you ready to engage? Then let's look at a few ideas that will help deep engagement create deep acceptance and, as a result, speed implementation of your do-ONE THING-deep engagement campaign.

Decide the approach

Decide your approach early. Consider what will be the appropriate level of engagement for your ONE THING campaign. Then look at how some (or possibly all) of the following scale of approaches can work for you.

- **Inform** – tell people what you are doing and why
- **Consult** – seek feedback through one of many possible mechanisms
- **Involve** – include the group, their aspirations and concerns in planning and decision making
- **Collaborate** – actively support participation in every aspect of the initiative
- **Empower** – enable people to take charge and do it themselves with support from experts.[97]

Each of these approaches will be useful in some context. Indeed, a *do*-ONE THING-*deep* engagement campaign might not have a single approach. Some aspects might require different levels of engagement. But ideally, aim just slightly higher than you think is practically possible. Support more than just simple participation and seek to enable agency. Whatever the initiative is, these are great goals to have.

Get people on board

Know your market – your people. Who will be hearing your ONE THING message? How will you take it to a place where those people can use it and in a form they understand? How will you ensure they have a voice in the creation and experience of the *do*-ONE THING-*deep* journey? If you are able to facilitate a conversation in your organisation among people and leaders about your message, you'll get a great outcome. But to do this, you are going to need people with a mix of skills and perspectives to help.

So how do you go about getting the right people on board? There is no one right way, but there are a few things to keep in mind when considering who to approach.

- **Enthusiastic advocates** – who will help you spread the message
- **Affected parties** – who have skin in the game and will be impacted by the initiative
- **Experts** – who have specialist knowledge or skills that will help with the initiative
- **Outsider perspective** – people who brings fresh eyes to your ONE THING.

There are also two other groups to consider. First, the latecomers. You will get people on board at different times. It can be useful to help these late adopters feel included and get them up to speed quickly. Maybe you can do this by finding people to support them or offer some great resources.

Second, the organisation's leaders. You need to keep inclusive engagement at the front of their minds for your ONE THING engagement campaign to succeed.

Align activities

How will you gather feedback from your people? How will you action the information they give you? At each step of the way, you will need to shape what you discover and incorporate it into the message. Include it in the broader marketing plan and keep leadership in the loop. The information you gather will provide you with the key points you need to further engaging your people, understand the messages that resonate and the best way to deliver them. How you go about involving people with the message and the plan will depend on your chosen engagement level. For example, you might:

- **Inform** – put out a message
- **Consult** – set up focus groups
- **Involve** – hold a facilitation session for feedback
- **Collaborate** – run a strategy, brainstorm or design a workshop
- **Empower** – ask the group what support they need.[98]

There are so many ways to do this. Think about creating the right environment for discovery. If you need to bring people on to support this, do so, because facilitating engagement effectively is a skill. It might be good to have someone experienced and independent to support engagement. It can be hard to bring up tricky matters within an established group. There may be preconceptions, likes and dislikes, so having someone external can help overcome inherent biases. Like any human being, these outsiders will bring their own biases to the table too, but an expert facilitator is more aware than most of where these can pop up and how they need to deal with them.

Outside expertise in managing personalities, getting a good understanding of what's happening in the room and bringing out valuable insights will help you and your team get excellent outcomes. Experts also have a bagful of engagement tools to make the sessions fun and productive. Their level of skill and their perceived independence will make the investment worthwhile.

Armed with a range of ideas and information, keep feeding the loop so that leaders and your message are aligned and singing your do-ONE THING-deep song.

Manage the team

As the engagement continues, you'll start to see the plan in motion. A couple of unexpected things may occur and need to be managed, but that's not unusual. Hopefully, the group members are inspired by the ONE THING's purpose and will assist in resolving any issues. If they become increasingly motivated as a result of their involvement, they'll enthusiastically engage with getting done what needs doing.

However, it is not unheard of (she says generously) that all kinds of human foibles can get in the way of making THINGs happen. Here are a few examples:

- Big picture thinkers and planners don't see implementation as their job.

- Perfectionists don't like how others work, and the need to do everything themselves becomes burdensome. They alienate others who are keen to contribute. Eventually, they feel resentful.

- Those actively and regularly working on the implementation feel put upon by people they believe aren't pulling their weight.

Leaders need to keep a keen eye on where conflict or dissatisfaction sits just below the surface. Addressing tension, managing expectations and communicating effectively within the group will keep things on track. There is no room for head-in-the-sand leadership. What's needed is to be proactive in creating environments where such behaviours don't flourish, especially at the 'collaborate' and 'empower' levels of engagement where diverse ideas are encouraged.

Take action

Anthropologist Margaret Mead said, 'Never doubt that a small group of thoughtful, committed citizens can change the world: indeed, it's the only thing that ever has.'[99] Here we are deep in the 'doing' part of our ONE THING engagement campaign. Connecting with people who are sharing information, ideas and forming ongoing actions is part of the campaign. So keep working the plan – keep collecting and incorporating the information you and your team gather.

If keeping on top of this proves challenging, support with data collection and analysis can be valuable when working on any major ONE THING. This is a specialised skill that is not available in every organisation. Consider engaging an expert who will limit bias and misperception in the design and collection of information, and who can understand how to analyse and interpret the data. This increases your organisation's trust in the fairness of the process and the validity of the resulting analysis.

And throughout this time, remember to keep focused on the Principles of Deep. Check that there is sufficient time and a variety of approaches to help everyone feel they have an opportunity to engage with the ONE THING in a meaningful way.

Fully engaged ONE THING

Nothing beats working together and sharing the joys and challenges of a meaningful project. It's more than reaching an outcome. It's an opportunity to build greater connection and trust. The strengthening of social bonds in teams, organisations and communities has been shown to have positive health-giving effects to those involved.[100]

Today, many social and political factors are playing out in a world that is arguably more divided than ever. Now this may sound hyperbolic, but getting this ONE THING right is a gift to the world. Helping people work well with those they may not otherwise choose to, or have the opportunity to get to know up close and personal, is an opportunity for healing division.

That's why thinking through your approach and engaging external expertise to support engagement in your ONE THING can be worthwhile. Expressing opinions, hearing and understanding those different from you, valuing the experience and knowledge people can bring to the table are skills for a better future. A strong ONE THING engagement campaign is worth investing in.

CHAPTER 11
THE MARKETING CAMPAIGN

Marketing is a contest for people's attention.[101]

SETH GODIN

In this, our final campaign, we focus on marketing as a vital part of the *do*-ONE THING-*deep* experience. Marketing will likely be the most visible aspect of your organisation's ONE THING campaign.

Any *do*-ONE THING-*deep* campaign's marketing ideas, created in tandem with the engagement campaign, need to be relevant, meaningful and well crafted. The stories they tell will need to resonate with your people to support the changes you want to see. Getting this right is critical. A significant aspect of your initiative's success will stem from how well you sell your message. It needs to have an impact on, and influence, your people.

Remember, you are looking to keep your organisation's ONE THING on everyone's desk and front of mind, rather than it being discarded or paid lip-service to and not actioned. As I've said earlier, that means it must be **clear** (easy to understand), **simple** (easy to do) and **sticky** (easy to recall and share).

Marketing campaigns, like political campaigns, come with their own stigma. For some people it brings up the image of a sleazy salesperson – someone trying to convince them to buy something they don't need for a problem they didn't know they had but now feel pretty insecure about. It's the loud, shouty ads on telly that are just plain annoying. It's the interrupting sales call as you are trying to cook dinner and the spam in your inbox. All that sort of thing makes us feel icky and keeps us on guard for unscrupulous people selling expensive oils extracted from exotic snakes.

Sales and marketing have changed significantly, especially with the invention of the interweb and the ubiquity of smartphones. People are moving away from traditional forms of marketing to engage with products on their devices.[102] There is more opportunity to research products and that is seen as an advantage for consumers. Armed with increased knowledge, buyers now have the upper hand rather than the seller. It appears that, 'We don't sell anymore. People buy.'[103]

There is a famous marketing adage that says, 'People don't want to buy a quarter-inch drill, they want to buy a quarter-inch hole!'[104] If this is even a little bit true, it astounds me that every company about to go through a digital transformation – and who isn't? – doesn't capitalise on this. Instead of focusing on the new shiny technology, you could work with the organisation in a broader 'work smarter' campaign, for example. Aligning the organisation's values or mission, engaging its people early, working broadly and beyond the tech, and taking the focus off the system and onto the outcomes – that sounds like working smart to me.

Marketing guru Seth Godin tells us that:

Marketers make change happen. If you can make someone better, if you can open a door for someone, if you can shine a light, that's an act of marketing. Because what you've done is brought an idea of a product or a service to someone who needs it, and offered them help.[105]

A marketing campaign is a way to promote awareness of a brand, product or service using a range of media – print, television, radio, online platforms and other techniques.[106] Rich Silverstein, co-chair and partner at GS&P (Goodby, Silverstein & Partners),[107] an award-winning creative agency with branches in San Francisco and New York, describes a great marketing campaign as one where 'everything speaks to the same idea. But it just gets better and better and better. And the public really feels connected to it.' [108]

Now that sounds like doing ONE THING deep.

So if marketing isn't slimy and loud and instead aims to make a positive change in a way that everyone feels personally engaged with, what would that look like? How can you bring a positive marketing mindset to your ONE THING? How can you and your organisation get your message across effectively? Let's check out a few key points to consider while on the marketing campaign trail.

Message

COMMIT
Accept the brief.

LISTEN
Know your market.

SAY
Plan your kick-arse message.

DO
Build, test, deploy.

PLAY
Make it happen.

DESTINATION
Message received.

Accept the brief

Deciding to accept this brief means understanding the campaign's goals, the expected engagement level, and how you will be working with your organisation's leaders, employees and those involved in the project to activate this ONE THING.

When thinking about the 'message' of a *do*-ONE THING-*deep* marketing campaign, it needs to be more than merely a slogan or comms. These are important, but for a ONE THING campaign, it's useful to broaden the definition and include any way information needs to be shared. It can be anything that involves growing awareness and understanding that changes behaviour. This could mean comms, professional development, events, realigning processes and knowledge management. The message is not just something you hand over to the communications team, it's part of the engagement and will involve a range of business functions.

Know your market

One of the most influential thinkers on management, Peter Drucker, tells us that marketing will reduce the need for selling. But this happens only if we 'know and understand the customer so well that the product or service fits him and sells itself'.[109]

No matter how good your message, your campaign's delivery or the involvement of your leaders are, they will fail without a good understanding of the market. Luckily, we have our engagement campaign to help. But let's be clear, there is never one market. There are many. You need to know who you want to influence, how they like to receive messages, and account for different age groups, personalities and thinking preferences. This means looking at different marketing modes, platforms and styles of delivery.

Does your market – or a part of your market – respond to data, facts and statistics? Does your demographic prefer stories and look for a more emotional connection? Do you need to interact with your audience online or face-to-face? Or via written, visual, text-based, video, long-form, short-form, email, web or app information? The choices of how you present your material are endless. But your approach will come down to who your customers are, where they hang out so the message gets to them and what their preferred information looks like. Build some avatars or personas, if that is helpful, but flesh out who you are engaging by doing your research.

Don't overlook the leaders in your organisation who will be acting as sponsors for your ONE THING. Gain a good understanding of their individual communication styles. Play to their strengths. Get them some help if they need to stretch beyond their current communications capabilities. They will be taking essential aspects of the message to the organisation. There is no point asking them to sing if they are dancers. (Sorry, that was the best metaphor I could come up with.)

Plan your kick-arse message

You are clear on the goal, you know the people, you understand the strengths and interests that will drive this ONE THING. Now build it, and they will come. Not every person in the organisation, not all at once, but your people *will* join your *do*-ONE THING-*deep* campaign – over time and deeply. That's the plan. Now it's time to get creative. Map out the approach and nail the message that will get your people on board for this ONE THING journey. Yes, it's time to kick arse – and here's how to do it.

A sticky message

Make your ONE THING message:

- **Clear** – If it's easy to understand, people will get it!
- **Simple** – If it's easy to know what to do, people will want to act on it!
- **Sticky** – If it's easy to recall and share, people won't be able to shake it!

In Dan and Chip Heath's book *Made to Stick: Why some ideas survive and others die,*[110] these bestselling authors discuss how some ideas stick while others are forgettable. They define sticky ideas as those that are clearly understood, easily remembered and motivate action. One concept they discuss is 'Commander's Intent': a 'very short and simple sentence that sums up the overarching goal of the organisation and functions as a filter for localized decision making'.[111] Sounds very ONE THING to me.

But you could also think about our earlier examples: the British Rowing crew's, 'Will this make the boat go faster?' and my constant and useful refrain, 'Just do ONE THING' (hmm … catchy). Another oft-quoted example (featured in *Made to Stick*) is that of Southwest Airline's assertion, 'We are THE low fare airline.' This is a clear signal that flying with them will be a no-frills event. Then there's 'Better together.' Microsoft's APAC President Andrea Della Mattea saw a need for the regions to work as one team. They chose the phrase and then told stories in different media about how they already are better together, not how to become better together. The theme was so successful, they continued to use it at conferences for three years.[112]

Remember that even if you hire the best marketing experts in the world, it's likely that not everyone will like the ONE THING message when they first hear it. A few people may not ever like it. But you need to give it your best shot. Let deep do its work to give people time and some variety so they can fall in love with the message just a little.

A (mostly) flexible schedule

Keeping in mind that as this whole *do*-ONE THING-*deep* campaign will go over an extended time, you will want to spread out and mix up the campaign's approach and activities. The purpose of this is to continually build and refresh engagement with the ONE THING until it's business-as-usual. To do this, you will need a plan.

Schedule your key ONE THING events in advance, like your launch event, learning schedule, when you want to refresh the message and when you release materials. Think about any existing sessions and events you might want to co-opt for the good of your ONE THING, such as town halls. Call dibs in publications. Book time and people (and back-up people) for any planned events.

Map your schedule out carefully so everyone working in your

ONE THING marketing campaign team knows what they have to do by when. Alert leaders and employees to what's coming and what they need to do to be ready.

Just as important as planning, stay alert to what's happening in the organisation and be opportunistic about seizing ways to incorporate your message into what's going on. This is a great way to keep your ONE THING fresh and topical.

A bunch of resources

Your aim is to attract as many people as you can, so you will need various resources to convey your ONE THING message. Think about:

- **Your peoples' preferences** – different thinking, learning and communications styles

- **Your people's level of engagement** – how enthusiastic or resistant they are to change

- **Your leaders' preferences** – what they can do and what they will get behind

- **Your outcome** – what your ONE THING is asking your people to do differently

- **Your budget** – what you can afford, realistically, in terms of people, time and money

- **Your timeframe** – how long you can spend on this ONE THING.

So you've kicked arse with your message making. What do you need to build the campaign?

Build, test, deploy

Excellent. You've got the message, some ideas on how to get it out there in many different ways and a plan for doing it. It's all coming together. But you might also need some of the following:

- **Stuff** – such as a recognisable brand and some products to put it on

- **Content** – writing for speeches, flyers, newsletters - you know the drill

- **Events** – how you'll sell some sizzle, either through existing platforms or by creating something just for this ONE THING

- **Learning** – information, development and support that people can access when honing their ONE THING skills

- **Touchpoints** – recognising how your ONE THING fits into key aspects of the employee experience, like recruitment, induction, performance, etc.

Keep testing your ideas and seeking feedback. Some good engagement at this point will help you feel more confident in your approach, help spread the word and keep everyone motivated. If certain aspects of the campaign don't receive good feedback, they might need to be quickly and quietly retired. Perhaps they will be more valuable down the track, or maybe it's just bye-bye.

Make it happen

It's planned, we are ready, people are getting excited, let's go. Now it's about keeping everyone on track and working on the plan. It's helpful to think global and encourage local. How can specific project teams, sites and departments start to make this *do*-ONE THING-*deep* campaign their own? If you are getting this process right, you will now need to loosen the reins and see where it can go.

Work closely and continuously with the sponsors. Leaders grossly underestimate how often you have to repeat a message for people to hear it and then to have it seen as 'just how we do things now'. There needs to be a focus on keeping leaders informed, sometimes gently poking them with a motivation stick, and helping them be their best. Sometimes you will just be trying to keep them on message. (Cat herding, anyone?)

Also, have fun. This should be hard work that is enjoyable for everyone working on the marketing campaign. And a word of caution for everyone who is actively working in the *do*-ONE THING-*deep* project team. Just don't make it all about you. These are special initiatives and not everyone will be hands on in these teams. I have watched project teams that love what they do inadvertently alienate parts of the organisation because they let this specialness go to their heads. Help others have fun and ensure they feel involved and heard. Ask yourself, could you give over that plum job you really wanted to someone else because you know it will have an enormous impact if you get them involved? I hope you could.

Message received

Soon, the message and initiatives should be starting to have an effect. There will be aggregate fluency for your ONE THING messages and activities and you will begin to see some positive changes. It is your role to start reflecting that back. Reinforce the successes of the ONE THING. Share your wins. For those late adopters to come over the line, they need to see that this isn't just all shine, but there is also depth and substance. Leaders are telling them this ONE THING matters. Colleagues are getting benefits from it. It's everywhere, it's not frightening and they can see how it fits into their working life.

By being open about some of the challenges that occur, people who are a little wobbly about getting on board will see that wobbly is something that happens and it's possible to get through it. There is no shame in trying and not getting it right the first time.

Let's recap

Your *do*-ONE THING-*deep* campaign needs to have people engaged and a great message that leaders actively promote. The people, the leaders and the message rely on each other to achieve the change sought for your ONE THING.

» To get your ONE THING moving, we need to adopt a campaign mindset and let the Principles of Deep work for you.

» Heed the learnings from great political, engagement and marketing campaigns to build a well balanced campaign.

» Campaigns come in all shapes and sizes so it might be big and loud or small and subtle, and while it will be shiny and novel to catch people attentions it will also be baked into the everyday experience of the work.

» On the campaign trail, remember to commit, listen, say, do and play. Put all of these together and you and your people will arrive at your destination and be better for the journey.

Now, to illustrate what a *do*-ONE THING-*deep* campaign looks like up close and personal, let's share a ONE THING fable told through the eyes of a leader who is a novice campaigner.

PART 5
A DO-ONE THING-DEEP FABLE

*Storytelling is the most powerful way to put
ideas into the world today.*[113]

ROBERT MCKEE

I have a confession to make. I'm not always a fan of fables in business literature. I know lots of people love them, but with a few notable exceptions, I tend to skip these parts of a book – the case studies neatly segregated from the flow of the text, the personal examples. I'm usually keen to get on with the meatier ideas that flow through the main body of the work. But in this instance, I'd obviously advise against doing that. Fables can be a bit naff, but this one isn't.

It is a hopeful tale of a leader's journey to ONE THING-ness. And while this is strictly fictional, as fables are, it comes from observations, lived experience and missed opportunities collected throughout my working life. So pull up a chair near the fire, settle in with a nice cup of cocoa (or an excellent brandy), and be taken away to the wonderful world of doing ONE THING deep.

CHAPTER 12
A ONE THING LEADERSHIP FABLE

Attention is the currency of leadership.[114]

RONALD A HEIFETZ

Sitting in a sunny spot in the café near work, I'm checking a few messages, enjoying a coffee and a rare quiet moment before I have to leave for a meeting. A very chatty trio come in and sit down at the table behind me. I can hear they are employees at the organisation I lead, but I can't see who they are.

'It's hard to know why we bother,' one of them says.

'Agreed. What happened with last year's survey? We filled it out, we got a lecture from that consultant on how crap we were. They came up with some lame actions and never thought about it again.'

'It does seem pretty pointless.'

'And they're not cheap to run. Especially if nothing happens as a result.'

'There is so much going on. Who's got time for surveys anyway? And nothing ever changes.'

'But it could. And having some feedback from everyone on how we feel about our work could be valuable.'

'Dream on.'

'Okay, here's my dream then. We do the survey. The exec gets the results and uses them to pick ONE THING we can improve on as an organisation. Because we are busy, it will take us some time to work on it, but we could make one change. Not even a big one. We'd go deep and do it really well, not just some tick-the-box, quick and dirty reaction.'

'Can you hear me, Rover Three? This is Ground Control. You have left your orbit. Over.'

'You are loud and clear, Ground Control, but I'm not coming in just yet. If the organisation gets this right, people would see that it is possible to make a difference and everyone might not feel so cynical. Rover Three has faith in this. Over.'

'Ha! That all sounds like more work for us. And seriously, you know it won't help. I'm busy as it is, without all that malarkey. I'd like things to stay just as they are.'

The conversation shifted among the group. I found myself feeling defensive and annoyed. As I went to the counter to pay, I glanced over at their table and they looked a little shocked when they saw me. I only recognised one of the people in the group. It was Janice. I realised she had been the voice of hope about the possibilities for change.

What they spoke about festered in my mind all through and after my meeting. But on the way back to work, my thoughts slowly relaxed from angry defensiveness to curiosity. The last few quarters had been tough for our business. There had been plenty of unexpected events. But was that really an excuse? As the CEO, I couldn't clearly identify anything that was directly achieved because of last year's survey. Not that we hadn't achieved anything, but I couldn't make that connection. It was just more data that got rolled up into all the information that came my way every day. But I could see how it probably looked like a giant waste of time to those people we had asked to contribute.

The investigation

At the next exec meeting, I asked the team about the whole survey thing. How much did our survey cost last year? What was our participation rate? Was that result an upward or downward trend? When are we scheduling the next one?

Our CHRO[115] was able to share details of the process. When I asked about what last year's actions were following the survey and how we reported them, there was a lot of mumbling.

'Something about bullying.'

'Outcomes included in the strategy.'

'No separate outcomes report.'

'Didn't comms handle that?'

These were just some of the lacklustre responses.

And what were the actions for each of their departments? A mixed response. Some remembered, others didn't, with the latter looking a little sheepish.

'I'm not trying to attribute blame here,' I said. 'I'm just curious.'

I was beginning to see why our people were reluctant to engage and had low expectations around change. I shared the conversation I overheard the previous day with the group and, not unlike my initial response, they were a little defensive. Still, it was clear that something needed to be done.

'I think maybe we do need to have ONE THING that we focus on this year so that we can show people this survey matters, that we are listening. I'm not expecting us to turn participation and engagement around overnight. But maybe over the next couple of years, we can demonstrate that the money we spend on asking the staff what they think is actually put to use. Hopefully, that will start to shift some of the concerns they have, which we probably share too.'

My suggestion was followed by a race to come up with ideas and solutions there and then. While I appreciated their suggestions, that's not what I wanted. Instead, I asked each member of my leadership team to speak to their managers and any employees they happen to meet with over the next couple of weeks. Talk to people informally, with curiosity and a desire to understand. Then they could tell me what people think about the survey. And perhaps find out ONE THING that would make the process more worthwhile.

The listening tour

Two weeks later we held a special meeting. A trusted facilitator was engaged to delve into how the team went about gathering info and what they found out. Hearing about how the leadership team went about the process was as illuminating as what was discovered.

Employees failed to see the value, were in one of the few teams that used the results well, or said what they thought their managers expected to hear – albeit unconvincingly. For those who answered honestly, most said that when nothing came of the survey, it was perceived as a costly waste of time. 'People they knew' felt that it lessened trust in the organisation's leadership because, 'They ask for an opinion that they never consider.'

If we were to do a survey this year, I wanted to either change this perception and make it meaningful or ditch it until we could. We had to take responsibility for the failings of all the previous surveys and change our approach, one way or another.

Use it or lose it

Turns out we were already committed to the next survey. We had forked over the dough, so to speak. We were going ahead – but I wanted to make sure we did it a little differently.

I trusted HR and the survey company to demonstrate that we

were getting clean and accurate data. I was interested to see how we were planning to engage people and how we would use what we found out. Comms had a plan, HR had timelines for delivery and feedback sessions across the organisation. But I wanted more. I wanted everyone in my leadership team to be all over this. I saw it as a way to build our leadership skills and create a more connected group.

The idea I had overheard that afternoon in the café of doing ONE THING and doing it deep kept swirling around in my head. I asked Janice if she'd meet with me. I was honest about overhearing the conversation and told her that I thought she was right. If we were going to do another survey, how did she see it happening?

Janice's suggestions were to the point:

- Identify ONE THING that matters to enough people.

- Have activities run over a longer timeframe, so the people who are usually slow to get on board have enough time to see how it could work for them.

- Have various ways of getting the information and expectations out. This is important for those who adopt early and get bored, and also because we learn in different ways and need messages repeated and reinforced if they are to stay with us.

Then there was one other necessary factor. Janice was adamant that if this condition couldn't be met, there was no point in trying. She was clear that it was crucial for leaders to act as dedicated sponsors in this process.

Her emphasis on this last point made me curious. I asked her about her definition of a dedicated sponsor, and her expectations of what they should do.

She said that leaders needed to be seen to be acting in alignment with the change, recognising others who did this well and holding those falling below the line to account. And if this was going to be over an extended time, they needed to stay the course and help others do the same. The change needed to be something always on their mind, so they could take opportunities to wrap it into conversations around projects and how people in the organisation do their work. Janice explained that for her, strong leadership meant being across what was happening and speaking with one voice. There should be no miscommunication or niggly undermining. She gave some salient examples of where this had happened before – including, to my surprise, in my own leadership team.

That was certainly a lot to consider. But I had two more questions for Janice. 'How would you feel about writing all this in a proposal for me? And is there anything or anyone that you need to help you with that?'

Gathering the players

Thanks to that random encounter in the café, our *do*-ONE THING-*deep* campaign (as Janice referred to it) was underway. And 'deep' meant that we were going to focus on what people told us mattered to them and then involve our people in getting those things done. This was the part of the survey we had been missing – great implementation.

I took personal responsibility for the interdepartmental project team that would work on our do-ONE THING-deep campaign. I gathered those with the required skills and motivation and worked with them on the project. My presence and involvement meant that people saw I was taking this seriously. With me there, anyone in our meetings would feel the need to at least fake enthusiasm! Although if that was the case, I couldn't tell. Everyone seemed very positive and engaged.

And while I kept abreast of what was happening, I also maintained my focus on my leadership team. Without their sponsorship of our ONE THING, it would be just a lot of wasted oxygen and time. I knew I had to step up to lead my team through the next few months and instil a ONE THING mindset.

Clarifying expectations

The preparations were underway. There was considerable work ahead for those engaging our people and running and analysing the survey. In the meantime, I wanted to use the time to prepare my leadership team for their roles as sponsors. This was an opportunity for our team to focus, connect and develop our leadership.

When we first got together to discuss this, we did so without knowing what our ONE THING message would be. We knew we needed an umbrella idea that could be used for other key projects we did throughout the year. Our ONE THING implementation plan mapped out our existing programs and timeframes, and identified placeholders for activities that could be considered. Nothing was locked in. We also discussed other ways we could work together or within our departments on our ONE THING.

More importantly, we talked about the skills we would need to be great sponsors for our ONE THING throughout the year. We also did a premortem to identify what could get in the way of our team achieving this. We came up with a page full of answers to the question, 'Why won't this work?' It looked like we had our work cut out for us.

Allowed to voice concerns in the premortem, the team were able to clarify misconceptions. We had a list of things to consider when our ONE THING message was clear. However, if we were to do this process each year – choose ONE THING inspired by that year's survey and act on it – we also needed to identify and clarify what skills we needed to improve or learn as leaders of a ONE THING organisation.

While I was keen to invest in our development, I didn't want this to involve another off-site or public course where someone disappeared for a couple of days or weeks, then, on their return, found it impossible to put any of the great things they learned into practice. I'd seen this happen a number of times over the years, for different reasons. Sometimes it was because there was so much to do that the ideas just slipped away while managing everyday spot fires. Or the larger group wasn't aware of what had been learnt – or didn't understand the value of it – so the existing culture overpowered the opportunity for change.

Instead, I wanted us to work on *how* we worked *as* we worked. For us to have one focused objective for our leadership team and figure out a way to embrace opportunities and overcome challenges together. I liken this approach to one of those action learning projects popular in leadership development programs. While those projects are generally interesting, they are not always salient to the work being done at the time. This was right-here-right-now development. And we were doing it together.

What could possibly go wrong?

Our ONE THING

After what I overheard in the café that afternoon, the conversation that began this whole ONE THING, I wondered how I had let myself miss this. Half-jokingly, the thought, I need better listening skills, popped into my mind. Could this be something I would like to explore? I wondered how well we, as the leadership team, heard each other and connected. And what about how we worked with our people in the rest of the organisation? Did we listen to them well enough? Did we connect? Could thinking about this be a good place to start for our team, and would they be happy to explore it with me? Or was there something else we should do? Something more urgent, more important, or that just needed to be done first?

After sussing out interest in the team, we agreed that developing better listening skills was a useful area for us to work on. I sought some recommendations from our learning and development team about who was considered an expert in this area. After our initial session working with a listening skills specialist, who had great information and a practical approach for our team exploration, we were asked to set individual intentions for practising our slowly improving skills. My question was how we hold each other to account and give helpful feedback and support. It was at this point that one of our team felt incensed and lashed out at the process. In layman's terms, they spat the dummy.

Despite this, we had, apparently, been learning. We found ourselves able to ask this individual some questions and listen to their answers with curiosity and compassion. We all sought to understand what was going on. It was quite a lesson. Eventually, we uncovered a fear of judgement and a physical hearing impairment. Others who were struggling felt safe enough to discuss their lack of confidence with some of the new skills they had just learnt. And one person aired concerns about how not being the one with the answers might undermine the perception of them as a leader. I had rarely been prouder of our team. We listened, did not immediately seek to fix anything and, more importantly, came to understand that it might be okay to be vulnerable. Even after the unexpected outburst from our colleague, there was nothing but support. I felt something shift that day.

The message

The results were in. We had raised our participation level in the survey by engaging with our team and sharing our plans to do ONE THING and do it deep. Our people cautiously respected our approach because we clearly articulated our intention to take action and not overwhelm them with well-meaning but superficial initiatives. We didn't promise to get it right every time, but we could try to make a difference together. Following a debriefing from our survey provider on the outcomes, we recognised there were lots of potential areas to explore. So now we needed to choose our ONE THING. To do this, we had to take the survey data, the things we knew that were already in our strategy and the organisation's environmental factors into account – then decide.

After the session that morning, I invited Janice to meet and reflect on how we were tracking and what was ahead. We agreed that it was rubber-hitting-the-road time. Over coffee, Janice shared with me a recent conversation she'd had with her team members after achieving a difficult goal. She had complimented them by saying they were like bamboo. Initially, they'd taken offence. Bamboo is difficult to control and could get out of hand, right? But Janice explained it was their strength, resilience and focus on sustainability that she'd admired – all part of the bamboo profile.

Then Janice pulled something out of her bag to show me. It was a t-shirt with the words 'Be like bamboo' on the front. She'd had them made for her team. Apparently, they had adopted the phrase as a motto. (Although she confessed to not fully understanding the team's other saying, 'Beware the panda' ...)

After the year we had experienced, I wondered if this would work for the broader organisation. It fitted with critical aspects of the survey results. The leadership team decided to include it in a selection of messages we put to our people to vote on in a poll. The winning message would lead our ONE THING campaign. Now if

Do ONE THING and Do It Deep

you had told me that 'Be like bamboo' would be our ONE THING, I would have called you crazy. But it won the ballot by a goodly margin and suited our industry and our goals. Coincidentally, we had recently installed a new garden on three of our sites that all included large stands of native bamboo. The next step was to see what we, together as a united organisation, could make of our ONE THING over the coming year.

Setting the example

With our ONE THING focus announced, planning and consultation got underway. I got back to my leadership team, who needed to understand the key message and what that meant for their sponsorship. We needed to identify how we could lead in a way that:

- developed strong connections
- supported a resilient workplace
- thought long-term and acted sustainably.

With that in mind, what actions would align with our 'Be like bamboo' agenda? How could we maintain behaviours that become consistent with our message?

The first few months of our *do*-ONE THING-*deep* journey was focused on developing stronger connections. And while these plans were unfolding, we needed to look at how our own team worked. How were we working well already and what got in our way? What could we strive for and what could we continue to tolerate despite less than perfect outcomes?

I was surprised by how open the team was now to sharing feedback, knowing they wouldn't be judged before being heard. There was some self-reflection on where we may need to deepen our own capabilities. As we looked at whether we could find the time to schedule regular discussions on this in our executive leadership meetings, my deputy pointed out, 'What could be more important than our culture?' We knew our own behaviour had to be above reproach, but we also needed to hold others in the organisation to account or be ready to praise excellence.

Outcome

This development took time, but it did not overtake our busy workload. It aligned with our work and focused on specific, timely and manageable activities. Over the months, I saw my leadership team deepen their connection and become less fearful in contradicting and evaluating opinions – without the need to take offence. People began to comment on a sense of greater trust amongst the leadership team and how it was starting to extend into their individual departments. The work we were doing in the organisation on our *do*-ONE THING-*deep* campaign was also delivering profound effects. And each leader was able to find different ways to check in with employees on how they thought this was going.

Not all of the activities, events and learning opportunities worked brilliantly, but we owned up and bounced back. Not every leader stayed completely above the line, but they were supported to be more buoyant where line issues were involved. Not every employee was convinced of our sincerity, but, over time, we got most people on board. It helped that this process was light-hearted but still taken very seriously by my team.

Surprisingly, across the twelve months, we never grew bored with 'Being like bamboo'. If anything, we became more involved, committed and came to see it as a valuable part of our work. We revelled in how all aspects of the message came to life and how other teams in the organisation made 'Be like bamboo' their own. Somewhere along the way, as our first ONE THING began to gather momentum, we noticed that enthusiasm for our ONE THING became infectious and self-sustaining.

We tracked a positive shift in the simple measures we set up for our ONE THING. We were more productive and engaged. But the outcomes went beyond that. There was a sense of trust and connection that I would not have expected could develop that quickly. There was still a way to go, but our workplace seemed happier, and the majority of our people more creative and engaged with their work.

I was so grateful to have overheard that conversation all those months ago. As a result, we became an organisation that was on a sustainable journey of growth. This outcome was personally and professionally very rewarding. As a leader of an organisation who took pride in serving its clients and supporting its people, I knew that this positive growth was ONE THING that would continue.

Reflecting on our successful ONE THING journey, I couldn't help pondering what our next do-ONE THING-deep campaign would look like. Whatever it would be, I knew that we had the know-how to make it work.

Let's recap

Hopefully, our fable was enlightening about what it takes to do a *do*-ONE THING-*deep* journey and lead a campaign. Here a few key ideas.

» Align the message, the engagement and the leadership in a campaign. This will slowly and deliberately change the organisation's culture.

» A ONE THING campaign should focus on the 'how' you work and be woven into daily rituals and significant events in the workplace. It's not down tools and only doing the ONE THING.

» A great campaign has a clear, concise and sticky message that is meaningful. This will result in it being understood and embraced by the majority of the organisation's people.

» There must be a deep engagement from employees. This builds a sound basis for trust.

» Leaders should take the opportunity that doing ONE THING deep provides to step up in their leadership role. It's the perfect way to learn about themselves and the people who make things happen in the organisation.

» Above all, make your *do*-ONE THING-*deep* journey fun ... it's gotta be a bit fun!

CONCLUSION

Somewhere inside of all of us is the power to change the world.[116]

ROALD DAHL

So you and your organisation have successfully implemented its ONE THING and, with a positive outcome, everyone is ready for the next one. But what is it that makes this process work? By focusing your organisation on ONE THING and doing it deeply – engaging everyone in something meaningful and delivering the message in different ways over time – you wisely invest in your most precious resource. Okay, I did say at the beginning of this book it was your people, but no, not your people ... how cliched. You engage the *attention* of your people. And where attention goes, energy follows. This is the secret to ONE THING success: **harnessing your people's**

attention. With this powerful source of energy, it's possible to implement a collaborative intention around something of substance that can potentially benefit the culture of the whole organisation.

One last recap

Do you recognise the signs? Are you working in an organisation that is stuck, fearful and unable to take action? Or overwhelmed with multiple priorities? Maybe it's time to do ONE THING and do it deep. Just remember:

» Whatever is going on at work, doing ONE THING is preferable to trying to do everything or doing nothing at all.

» Your ONE THING should be meaningful, memorable and relevant.

» Harness the energy in your organisation that is lost to overwhelm or apathy and redirect it in service of greater organisational health, achievement and the world we hope to create.

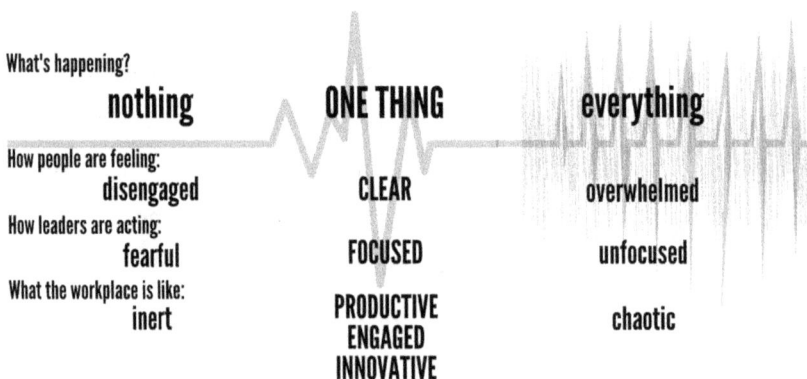

What's happening?		
nothing	**ONE THING**	**everything**
How people are feeling:		
disengaged	**CLEAR**	**overwhelmed**
How leaders are acting:		
fearful	**FOCUSED**	**unfocused**
What the workplace is like:		
inert	**PRODUCTIVE ENGAGED INNOVATIVE**	**chaotic**

The title of this book highlights the key things to focus on. The need for action – *Doing*; the need for focusing on what matters – **ONE THING**; and the need for giving it a red-hot go – *Deep*.

Doing

Be aware that anyone can get trapped by the desire to overachieve. It's easy to get sucked into the Every-THING workplace, doing lots but not doing ONE THING well. At the other end of the spectrum, we can also get paralysed by fear and end up stuck in a No-THING workplace, where no ONE THING is ever completed. Remember: successful 'doing' requires an ability to prioritise, commitment to the task and, above all, the courage to take a risk.

ONE THING

Leadership expert Matt Church says that the work of a leader is to 'replace fear with confidence, replace confusion with clarity, and mobilise people in pursuit of a better future'.[117] Focusing attention on doing ONE THING deep is that work.

People in any organisation seek clarity, purposeful work and connection. Stop wasting your people's precious time and attention on things that don't matter. Instead, ask what is a worthwhile focus for their attention? And how can this attention achieve your business's goals? How can it help your workplace to improve its culture, foster engagement and learning, encourage great work and increase job satisfaction for your people?

Deep

When you identify the ONE THING in your organisation that needs to be worked on, apply the Principles of Deep. Help everyone to contribute what they can.

Do that by allowing time for everyone to get on board and find their way to change. Help them with messages that they will understand. Address their communication and thinking style, whether that's by telling stories, giving statistics or drawing a model. It's time to ditch the quick fix and do it deep. Life's too short for half-arsed. Don't waste people's time with just-for-show, tick-the-box or quick-and-dirty. It undermines everything else you try to do that might be important. Make a difference and kick arse.

Deep impact

You may be surprised to hear this from me, but there is definitely more than one thing to commend a ONE THING approach for your teams, leaders and organisations. Here are some to look out for.

The things you intended to happen

First, there are the **things you intended** to happen. These are the positive outcomes you identified that would result from a successful *do*-ONE THING-*deep* journey.

- **Developing skills** – The result of working on the specific capabilities, behaviours and knowledge that you wanted to deepen. There is always a lot you could choose to do, so many skills to develop. Having chosen your ONE THING, it's easier to see the benefits that focus can bring on improving your people's skills. Working *en masse* on ONE THING has a multiplier effect that sees its capability deepen exponentially.

- **Working smarter** – Finding better ways to work by refining processes, encouraging learning and stimulating an environment for connection and innovation means everyone works smarter. This creates opportunities for increased productivity and innovation.

- **Focusing on what matters** – Helping people see what really matters by bringing greater clarity of purpose and giving everyone the opportunity to see where they fit in the organisation improves workplace culture. It takes some courage to do this when there is so much to do, but it is worthwhile.

The unintended things

Then there are **the unintended (but equally satisfying) things** that doing ONE THING deep will make happen over time.

- **Improving organisational health** – The clarity of purpose when working on ONE THING helps to address the overwhelm of a busy-ness-addicted workplace and remedies the boredom of an overly risk-averse one. It increases your people's resilience, encourages a healthy team environment and fosters a more positive workplace culture. Assisting people to work together on ONE THING builds the sort of trust and connection that overcomes silos and divisions.

- **Increasing engagement** – Over time, trust in leadership, the ability for people to work together to overcome challenges and grasp opportunities, and the belief in an organisation's ability to change will grow. Building this kind of purposeful workplace will bring all the benefits of greater engagement. Your company will look more attractive to great employees, be able to keep them longer and deliver more and higher quality work.

Beyond work

Then there are the aspects that go **beyond work** and extend into the greater good for all our lives.

- **Leading well** – We know that there is greater trust in business than there is in the government or the media.[118] I'm not sure we should be all that proud. I feel we are grading on the curve. In any case, great leadership examples in our organisations could lead us to expect – perhaps demand – this in our communities and our governments. If this happens, the type of listening, influencing and engagement we experience in a ONE THING organisation may just seep out more broadly into the world and become our expectations.

- **Working together** – Learning to work for the common good with people whose views you may not share but who you can nevertheless respect has never been more needed than now. Any way we can strive to overcome division matters, and starting where you work is as good a place as any. It may be that the workplace is one of the few remaining arenas that can, albeit imperfectly, hold a space to enable some of the most important social discussions of our time.

- **Encouraging civility** – Ideally, one outcome from a ONE THING workplace would be working more compassionately. I would start with the minimum acceptable standard for a journey to a more compassionate workplace, civility and respect. Yes, there'll still be lines that will be crossed and need addressing. Not everything can be done perfectly and in every organisation. But every small dose of kindness in the world is a blessing.

Now you may say I'm a dreamer. This little program that encourages focusing organisations on ONE THING in order to bring them together to solve something that matters isn't necessarily going to change the world. But maybe it's a start – except it's not. It's a continuation of what's already happening. It builds on lots of other programs that have a similar intent in workplaces and communities around the world. If together we could help heal part of the division that ails our world, wouldn't you want to be part of that? Well, you're not the only one.

Ready to save the world

Let's get to it then. Let's save the world ONE THING, one leader, one team, one organisation at a time and then share what we learn. Let the positive practice that is doing ONE THING deep, then another ONE THING, and another, fuel our workplaces. Then let it fuel our imaginations and release the power and magic of focused attention on the world. No passengers. No prima donnas.[119] Everybody shows up as their best self, ready to work together.

ENDNOTES

1 Mary Oliver, 'Yes! No!', *White Pine: Poems and prose poems*, Harcourt Brace, San Diego, 1994.

2 https://www.azquotes.com/quote/1398468

3 Roy T Bennett, *The Light in the Heart*, Roy Bennett, 2016.

4 Vincent van Gogh, edited by Mark Roskill, *The Letters of Vincent Van Gogh*, Touchstone Books, New York, 2008.

5 Harriet Beveridge and Ben Hunt-Davis, *Will It Make The Boat Go Faster?: Olympic-winning strategies for everyday success*, Troubador Publishing, Leicester, 2011.

6 *Cal Newport, Deep Work: Rules for focused success in a distracted world*, Grand Central Publishing (Hachette Book Group), New York, 2016.

7 https://www.linguanaut.com/learn-japanese/sayings-and-proverbs.php

8 ' ... 65-75% of organizations identified employee overwhelm as an issue ...'. Vanessa Loder, '75% Of Companies Struggle with Overwhelmed Employees – Here are Three Tips to Cope', *Forbes* online, New Jersey, April 24, 2015.
https://www.forbes.com/sites/vanessaloder/2015/04/24/75-of-companies-struggle-with-overwhelmed-employees-here-are-three-tips-to-cope/#46c7645512e8

9 '... 41% of the division's professionals and 61% of its managers agreed or strongly agreed with the statement that there is "not enough time to get your job done".'
Erin L Kelly and Phyllis Moen, 'Fixing the Overload Problem at Work', *MIT Sloan Management Review Magazine*, online, Summer 2020 issue, Massachusetts, April 27, 2020.
https://sloanreview.mit.edu/article/fixing-the-overload-problem-at-work

10 Rob Cross, Reb Rebele and Adam Grant, 'Collaborative Overload', *Harvard Business Review Magazine,* online, January–February issue, Massachusetts, 2016. https://hbr.org/2016/01/collaborative-overload

11 Rose Hollister and Michael D Watkins, 'Too Many Projects', *Harvard Business Review Magazine,* online, September–October issue, Massachusetts, 2018. https://hbr.org/2018/09/too-many-projects

12 Elizabeth Grace Saunders, 'How to Work for a Boss Who Has a New Idea Every 5 Minutes', *Harvard Business Review,* online, Massachusetts, November 16, 2018. https://hbr.org/2018/11/how-to-work-for-a-boss-who-has-a-new-idea-every-5-minutes

13 Rob Cross, Reb Rebele and Adam Grant, 'Collaborative Overload', *Harvard Business Review Magazine,* online, January–February issue, Massachusetts, 2016. https://hbr.org/2016/01/collaborative-overload

14 Daniel J Levitin, 'Why the Modern World is Bad for Your Brain', *The Guardian,* online, Australian edition, Sydney, January 15, 2015. https://www.theguardian.com/science/2015/jan/18/modern-world-bad-for-brain-daniel-j-levitin-organized-mind-information-overload

15 Ibid.

16 Erin L Kelly, Phyllis Moen, 'Fixing the Overload Problem at Work', *MIT Sloan Management Review Magazine,* online, Summer 2020 issue, Massachusetts, April 27, 2020. https://sloanreview.mit.edu/article/fixing-the-overload-problem-at-work

17 Ibid.

18 https://www.psychology.org.au/for-the-public/Psychology-Topics/Stress-in-the-workplace

19 William James, *The Principles of Psychology* Vol. I, Henry Holt and Co, New York, 1890, pp 403-404. Internet Archive, uploaded September, 2006. https://archive.org/details/theprinciplesofp01jameuoft

20 Helen Garner, 'Read All About It: Helen Garner', Melbourne Writers Festival Digital, 2020.

21 University College London, 'Our Brains' Information Processing Capacity is Constrained by a Constant but Limited Energy Supply', *SciTechDaily,* August 3, 2020.

https://scitechdaily.com/our-brains-information-processing-capacity-is-constrained-by-a-constant-but-limited-energy-supply/

22 Garth Sundem, 'This is Your Brain on Multitasking', *Psychology Today*, online, New York, 2012
https://www.psychologytoday.com/us/blog/brain-trust/201202/is-your-brain-multitasking

23 Sofie Bates, 'A Decade of Data Reveals That Heavy Multitaskers Have Reduced Memory, Stanford Psychologist Says', *Stanford News*, online, Stanford, October 25, 2018.
https://news.stanford.edu/2018/10/25/decade-data-reveals-heavy-multitaskers-reduced-memory-psychologist-says/

24 Marla Tabaka, 'Multitasking in This Digital World is Killing Your Productivity, and Research Says There's Worse News', *Inc. Magazine*, online, New York, October 22, 2018.
https://www.inc.com/marla-tabaka/multitasking-in-this-digital-world-is-killing-your-productivity-research-says-theres-worse-news.html

25 Bob Sullivan and Hugh Thompson, 'Brain, interrupted', *The New York Times Sunday Review*, New York, May 3, 2013.
https://www.nytimes.com/2013/05/05/opinion/sunday/a-focus-on-distraction.html

26 Mark Murphy, 'Interruptions at Work Are Killing Your Productivity', *Forbes*, online, New Jersey, October 30, 2016.
https://www.forbes.com/sites/markmurphy/2016/10/30/interruptions-at-work-are-killing-your-productivity/?sh=28e2038f1689

27 Chris Wheeler, 'The 5 Biggest Biases that Affect Decision-Making', *NeuroLeadership Institute*, New York, April 9, 2019. https://neuroleadership.com/your-brain-at-work/seeds-model-biases-affect-decision-making/

28 Freek Vermeulen, 'In Business Strategy, Short-Term Gains Often Cause Long-term Problems', *Forbes*, online, New Jersey, April 17, 2018. https://www.forbes.com/sites/freekvermeulen/2018/04/17/in-business-strategy-short-term-gains-often-cause-long-term-problems/?sh=6efa1e326e53

29 Julie Battilana, Anne-Claire Pache, Metin Sengul and Marissa Kimsey, 'The Dual-Purpose Playbook', *Harvard Business Review Magazine* online, March–April issue, Massachusetts, 2019.
https://hbr.org/2019/03/the-dual-purpose-playbook

30 Brent Gleeson, 'The Silo Mentality: How to break down the barriers', *Forbes*, online, New Jersey, October 2, 2013.
https://www.forbes.com/sites/brentgleeson/2013/10/02/the-silo-mentality-how-to-break-down-the-barriers/?sh=66daf2448c7e

31 Voltaire, *Candide, or Optimism*, translated by Theo Cuffe, Penguin Classics series, Penguin UK, London, 2006. Originally published in 1759 by Cramer in Geneva.

32 CRISPR technology is a way to edit genes. https://www.livescience.com/58790-crispr-explained.html

33 Douglas LaBier PhD, 'Feeling Bored at Work? Three Reasons Why and What Can Free You', *Psychology Today,* online, New York, May 3, 2010. https://www.psychologytoday.com/us/blog/the-new-resilience/201005/feeling-bored-work-three-reasons-why-and-what-can-free-you

34 David Sturt and Todd Nordstrom, 'Bored at Work? Science Says That's a Good Thing', *Forbes*, online, New Jersey, May 24, 2018. https://www.forbes.com/sites/davidsturt/2018/05/24/bored-at-work-science-says-thats-a-good-thing/#5370bbb44c91

35 https://www.safeworkaustralia.gov.au/bullying

36 Melissa Lamson, 'You're Not Burnt-Out. You're Bored-Out', *Inc. Magazine* online, New York, June 7, 2018. https://www.inc.com/melissa-lamson/8-ways-to-conquer-bore-out.html

37 Kate Pickels, 'A Boring Job Really CAN Make You Brain Dead: Lack of stimulation "affects memory and concentration later in life"', *Daily Mail Australia,* online, Sydney, June 17, 2016. https://www.dailymail.co.uk/health/article-3646254/A-boring-job-really-make-brain-dead-Lack-stimulation-affects-memory-concentration-later-life.html

38 *Harvard Business Review*, 'The Culture Factor: Employee attitudes can make or break your business. Here's how to get everyone moving in the right direction.', *Harvard Business Review*, January–February issue, Massachusetts, 2018. https://store.hbr.org/product/harvard-business-review-january-february-2018/br1801?sku=BR1801-MAG-ENG

39 There are a number of articles about this out there. Here are a few examples:
    Ben Butler, 'Worse than ever': Australian bank culture has not improved since royal commission, staff say' *The Guardian,* online, Australian edition, Sydney, April 7, 2021. https://www.theguardian.com/australia-news/2021/apr/07/worse-than-ever-australian-bank-culture-has-not-improved-since-royal-commission-staff-say
    Girard Dorney, 'What the Royal Commission Report Says about Culture', *HRM,* online, Sydney, February 6, 2019. https://www.hrmonline.com.au/culture/royal-commission-report-culture/

Stefanie Bradley and Daniel Knoll, 'Culture and Governance in Financial Services Following the Royal Commission', *KPMG Australia*, February 7, 2019. https://home.kpmg/au/en/home/insights/2019/02/financial-services-royal-commission-culture-and-governance.html

40 Peter Mills, '12 Reasons Why Your Business Strategies Fail', *Business Insider Australia*, Sydney, May 15, 2018. https://www.businessinsider.com.au/why-business-strategies-fail-2018-5

41 Sharon Lebell, *The Art of Living: The classical manual of virtue, happiness and effectiveness – Epictetus*, Harper One, San Francisco, 2007.

42 Patrick M Lencioni, *The Advantage: Why organizational health trumps everything else in business*, 1st edition, Jossey-Bass, San Francisco, 2012, p. 77, pp 119-131.

43 Yes, he even calls one of the sections of this chapter 'One Thing'.

44 https://www.brainyquote.com/quotes/christopher_reeve_167081

45 Samuel Smiles, *Self-Help: With illustrations of conduct, and perseverance, 1897 edition*. Originally published in 1859. This volume can be read online at: https://www.gutenberg.org/files/935/935-h/935-h.htm

46 Garth Sundem, 'This is Your Brain on Multitasking', *Psychology Today*, online, New York, 2012 https://www.psychologytoday.com/us/blog/brain-trust/201202/is-your-brain-multitasking

47 Marla Tabaka, 'Multitasking in This Digital World is Killing Your Productivity, and Research Says There's Worse News', *Inc. Magazine*, online, New York, October 22, 2018. https://www.inc.com/marla-tabaka/multitasking-in-this-digital-world-is-killing-your-productivity-research-says-theres-worse-news.html

48 Attributed to Goethe by Johannes Falk in *Goethe aus näherm persönlichen Umgange dargestellt: Ein Nachgelassenes Werk*, Forgotten Books, London, 2018. Originally published in 1832. https://www.azquotes.com/quote/344069

49 Daniel Pink, 'Daniel Pink Teaches Sales and Persuasion', *MasterClass*, online learning, San Francisco, 2020. https://www.masterclass.com/classes/daniel-pink-teaches-sales-and-persuasion

50 Robert E Quinn and Anjan V Thakor, 'Creating a Purpose-Driven Organization', *Harvard Business Review Magazine*, online, July–August issue, Massachusetts, 2018. https://hbr.org/2018/07/creating-a-purpose-driven-organization

51 EY Global, 'Why Business Must Harness the Power of Purpose', *EY Global*, London, December 15, 2020. https://www.ey.com/en_gl/purpose/why-business-must-harness-the-power-of-purpose

52 Ibid.

53 Mindtools Content Team, 'Learning Styles: The models, myths and misconceptions – and what they mean for your learning', *Mindtools*, Edinburgh, 2016. https://www.mindtools.com/mnemlsty.html

54 David Rock, Heidi Grant and Jacqui Grey, 'Diverse Teams Feel Less Comfortable – and That's Why They Perform Better', *Harvard Business Review*, Cambridge, 2016. https://hbr.org/2016/09/diverse-teams-feel-less-comfortable-and-thats-why-they-perform-better

55 Heidi Grant PhD, Neuroleadership Summit, New York, 2017. This quote is from my own notes taken at the summit.

56 Khalil Smith, Heidi Grant and Kamila Sip, 'It's Possible (and Dangerous) to Be Over-inclusive', *Quartz at Work,* New York, September 11, 2018. https://qz.com/work/1385091/inclusion-can-go-too-far/

57 https://citatis.com/a35037/

58 https://www.brainyquote.com/quotes/henry_ford_384400

59 Marc Kaplan, Ben Dollar, Yves Van Durme, 'Shape Culture', Deloitte. Insights, New York, February 29, 2016. https://www2.deloitte.com/us/en/insights/focus/human-capital-trends/2016/impact-of-culture-on-business-strategy.html

60 Shellye Archambeau, '3 Strategies for CEOs to Improve Corporate Culture', *Entrepreneur Asia Pacific,* online, June 5, 2017. https://www.entrepreneur.com/article/295171

61 Marc Kaplan, Ben Dollar, Yves Van Durme, 'Shape Culture', Deloitte. Insights, New York, February 29, 2016. https://www2.deloitte.com/us/en/insights/focus/human-capital-trends/2016/impact-of-culture-on-business-strategy.html

62 Jacob Morgan, 'How Corporate Culture Impacts the Employee Experience', *Forbes,* online, New Jersey, December 10, 2015. https://www.forbes.com/sites/jacobmorgan/2015/12/10/how-corporate-culture-impacts-the-employee-experience/#5acc2e09787c

63 Ibid.

64 Ibid.

65 Shellye Archambeau, '3 Strategies for CEOs to Improve Corporate Culture', *Entrepreneur Asia Pacific,* online, June 5, 2017. https://www.entrepreneur.com/article/295171

66 Kalani Iwiula, 'A CEO's Impact on Culture and Performance', Human Synergistics® International, Chicago, September 6, 2017. https://www.humansynergistics.com/blog/culture-university/details/culture-university/2017/09/07/a-ceo-s-impact-on-culture-and-performance

67 https://www.mckinsey.com/featured-insights/leadership/changing-change-management#

68 Christopher Smith, 'Change Management Research vs. the 70% Failure Rate', *Change* blog, San Francisco, March 4, 2019. https://change.walkme.com/change-management-research/

69 Boris Groysberg, Jeremiah Lee, Jesse Price and J Yo-Jud Cheng, 'The Leader's Guide to Corporate Culture', *Harvard Business Review Magazine,* online, January–February issue, Massachusetts, 2018. https://hbr.org/2018/01/the-culture-factor

70 Rose Hollister and Michael D Watkins, 'Too Many Projects', *Harvard Business Review Magazine,* online, September–October issue, Massachusetts, 2018. https://hbr.org/2018/09/too-many-projects

71 Rodger Dean Duncan, 'Culture, Leadership, Performance: How Are They Linked?', *Forbes,* online, New Jersey, October 30, 2018. https://www.forbes.com/sites/rodgerdeanduncan/2018/10/30/culture-leadership-performance-how-are-they-linked/#9ea09065e448

72 Eleanor Roosevelt.

73 Patrick M Lencioni, The Advantage: *Why organizational health trumps everything else in business,* 1st edition, Jossey-Bass, San Francisco, 2012, p 119.

74 Edelman, '2020 Edelman Trust Barometer', *Edelman,* New York, January 19, 2020. https://www.edelman.com/trust/2020-trust-barometer

75 https://www.goalcast.com/2018/01/16/most-inspiring-zig-ziglar-quotes/

76 You think I might have done a google search on the title, right? Great minds ... Anyhow, Gary's is a great book and you should read it.

77 Gary Keller with Jay Papasan, *The One Thing: The surprisingly simple truth behind extraordinary results,* Bard Press, Portland, 2013.

78 In a letter to Joë Bousquet, 13 April, 1942. Simone Pétrement, *Simone Weil: A Life, translated by Raymond Rosenthal*, Pantheon Books, New York, 1976.

79 https://www.briantracy.com/blog/leadership-success/leadership-quotes-for-inspiration/

80 Tom Peters and Robert H. Waterman, In Search of Excellence: *Lessons from America's Best-Run Companies,* Harper & Row, New York,1982.

81 Patrick M Lencioni, *The Advantage: Why organizational health trumps everything else in business*, 1st edition, Jossey-Bass, San Francisco, 2012.

82 Marshall Goldsmith with Mark Reiter, *What Got You Here Won't Get You There: How successful people become even more successful*, Random House, New York, 2007. Audiobook.

83 Ibid.

84 Margaret J Wheatley, *Turning to One Another: Simple conversations to restore hope to the future*, Berrett-Koelhler Publishers Inc, San Francisco, 2002.

85 Edelman, '2020 Edelman Trust Barometer', *Edelman*, New York, January 19, 2020. https://www.edelman.com/trust/2020-trust-barometer

86 Dana Wilkie, 'Employee Engagement Surveys: Why Do Workers Distrust Them?', *Society for Human Resource Management (SHRM)*, Virginia, January 05, 2018. https://www.shrm.org/resourcesandtools/hr-topics/employee-relations/pages/employee-engagement-surveys.aspx

87 Lisa Bigelow, 'How CIOs Can Lead Organizational Culture', *Smarter With Gartner*, Connecticut, January 7, 2020. https://www.gartner.com/smarterwithgartner/how-cios-can-lead-organizational-culture/

88 Melody Barnes and Paul Schmitz, 'Community Engagement Matters (Now More Than Ever)', *Stanford Social Innovation Review,* online, Spring issue, Massachusetts, 2016. https://ssir.org/articles/entry/community_engagement_matters_now_more_than_ever

89 Tim Moore, Myfanwy McDonald, Harriet McHugh-Dillon and Sue West, 'Community Engagement: A key strategy for improving outcomes for Australian families', *Australian Government Australian Institute of Family Studies*, CFCA Paper No. 39, Melbourne, April 2016. https://aifs.gov.au/cfca/publications/community-engagement/why-community-engagement-important

90 Ibid.

91 Brook Manville, 'Six Leadership Practices for "Wicked" Problem Solving', *Forbes,* online, New Jersey, May 15, 2016.

https://www.forbes.com/sites/brookmanville/2016/05/15/six-leadership-practices-for-wicked-problem-solving/#3bfe6fb3506b

92 Geelong Citizens, 'Geelong Citizens' Jury FAQs', Victoria State Government website, Melbourne. Page last updated September 9, 2019. https://www.localgovernment.vic.gov.au/our-programs/geelong-citizens-jury/frequently-asked-questions

93 This is currently being implemented as part of the Local government Act 2020 – see https://www.legislation.vic.gov.au/in-force/acts/local-government-act-2020/003 – albeit with some concerns over how this will emerge in practice. See: https://onlinelibrary.wiley.com/doi/10.1111/1467-8500.12420

94 Angela Priestley, 'Research Finds Diversity Leads to Better Decision-making', SmartCompany, Melbourne, September 27, 2017. https://www.smartcompany.com.au/people-human-resources/diversity-better-decision-making/

95 Stephanie N Downey, Lisa van der Werff, Kecia M Thomas, Victoria C Plaut, 'The Role of Diversity Practices and Inclusion in Promoting Trust and Employee Engagement', *Journal of Applied Social Psychology*, Vol. 45, Issue 1, 2015, pp 35–44. Excerpt featured on Deloitte. website. https://www2.deloitte.com/au/en/pages/human-capital/articles/role-diversity-practices-inclusion-trust-employee-engagement.html

96 Vivian Hunt, Dennis Layton and Sara Prince, 'Why Diversity Matters', McKinsey & Company, New York, January 1, 2015. https://www.mckinsey.com/business-functions/organization/our-insights/why-diversity-matters

97 Melody Barnes and Paul Schmitz, 'Community Engagement Matters (Now More Than Ever)', *Stanford Social Innovation Review,* online, Spring issue, Massachusetts, 2016. https://ssir.org/articles/entry/community_engagement_matters_now_more_than_ever#

98 IAP2 Federation, 'IAP2's Public Participation Spectrum', IAP2 International Association for Public Participation, 2014. https://www.iap2.org.au/wp-content/uploads/2019/07/IAP2_Public_Participation_Spectrum.pdf

99 Nancy C Lutkehaus, Margaret Mead: *The making of an American icon,* Princeton University Press, New Jersey, 2008, p. 261.

100 Tim Moore, Myfanwy McDonald, Harriet McHugh-Dillon and Sue West, 'Community Engagement: A key strategy for improving outcomes for Australian families', *Australian Government Australian Institute of Family Studies*, CFCA Paper No. 39, Melbourne, April 2016.

https://aifs.gov.au/cfca/publications/community-engagement/why-community-engagement-important

101 Seth Godin, *Purple Cow: Transform your business by being remarkable*, Portfolio (Penguin Group), New York, 2003.

102 Matthew Johnston, 'Smartphones Are Changing Advertising & Marketing', *Investopedia*, New York, March 26, 2020. https://www.investopedia.com/articles/personal-finance/062315/how-smartphones-are-changing-advertising-marketing.asp

103 Peter Cook, Michael Henderson and Matt Church, *Conviction: How thought leaders influence commercial conversations*, Thought Leaders Publishing, Balgowlah, 2012.

104 Theodore Levitt, *Marketing Myopia*, Harvard Business Review Press, Boston, 2008 (originally published in 1960). Listed in HBR's 10 Must Reads: The Essentials – An Introduction to the most enduring ideas on management from Harvard Business Review, Harvard Business Review Press, Boston, 2010.

105 Entrepreneur Marie Forleo blogs about her interview with Seth Godin here: https://www.marieforleo.com/2018/11/seth-godin-marketing/ and you can watch the interview here: https://www.youtube.com/watch?v=9YFNgKwv31A

106 Evan Tarver, 'Marketing Campaign', Investopedia, New York, December 01, 2020. https://www.investopedia.com/terms/m/marketing-campaign.asp#

107 https://goodbysilverstein.com/ This agency aims to 'create experiences that reach millions and even billions, but seem to speak only to you. We call this effect "mass intimacy".' Mass intimacy might be an ambitious aim for a ONE THING campaign. Maybe it's only something created by the most talented agencies with decades of experience – but it can't hurt to try.

108 https://www.masterclass.com/classes/jeff-goodby-and-rich-silverstein-teach-advertising-and-creativity/chapters/anatomy-of-a-campaign#

109 Peter F Drucker, *Managing Oneself*, Harvard Business Review Press, Boston, 2008. Originally published as an article in HBR, 1999. Listed in HBR's 10 Must Reads: The Essentials – An Introduction to the most enduring ideas on management from Harvard Business Review, Harvard Business Review Press, Boston, 2010.

110 Chip Heath and Dan Heath, *Made to Stick: Why some ideas survive and others die*, Random House, New York, 2007.

111 Lucio Buffalmano, 'Made to Stick Summary & Review', *The Power Moves*, January 3, 2018. https://thepowermoves.com/made-stick-summary

112 Storifying Events webinar, Anecdote, 30/9/2020.

113 https://mckeestory.com/is-it-possible-to-bring-storytelling-into-marketing/

114 Ronald A Heifetz, *Leadership Without Easy Answers*, Harvard University Press, Boston, 2009.

115 Chief Human Resources Officer.

116 Roald Dahl, *Matilda*, Jonathon Cape, London, 1988.

117 Matt Church, *Amplifiers: The power of motivational leadership to inspire and influence*, Wiley, Milton, 2013.

118 Edelman, '2020 Edelman Trust Barometer', *Edelman*, New York, January 19, 2020.
     https://www.edelman.com/trust/2021-trust-barometer

119 Not sure where I heard this, or if I made it up, but I think it was at a Blood, Sweat and Tears concert.

INDEX

diverse opinions 58
doing ONE THING 91, 95, 111, 117, 122, 153
    after another 51
    at a time 50
    deep 53-65, 154-7
    first 50
    for someone 52
    in different ways 57
    now 50
    over time 56
    quickly 51
    that matters 54-5
    with others 58

E

Edelman Trust Survey 107-8
employee engagement 107-18
employee surveys 36-7, 136-9
empowerment 112, 114
engagement 17, 40, 41, 76, 107-18
    approach 112
    collaboration 112, 114
    community 108-9
    deliberate 76
    employees 108-18, 150
    empowerment 112, 114
    evidence for 108-9
    facilitating 115
    increasing 156
    informing 112, 114
    involvement 112, 114
    lack of 76, 84
    marketing campaign 127
engagement campaign 88, 107-18
    aligning activities 114-15
    approach 112
    commitment 111
    consultation 109-12, 114, 138, 147
    evidence 108-9
    fully engaged ONE THING 117-18
    getting people on board 113
    knowing your market 113
    listening 111, 139

'open source' methodology 108
    taking action 116-17
    team management 115-16
    wicked problems 109
engagement/culture/climate/pulse/ staff survey 36-7
enthusiastic advocates 113
events 128, 148
Every-THING workplace 17, 19-29, 43, 75, 152
    addiction to activity 75
    attention 23-5
    multitasking 27-8
    physical and psychological harm 22
    pressures of 21-2
expectations 108, 142-4
experts 113

F

fables 133
failure of ONE THING 75-8
failure to allow enough time 78
fear of judgement 145, 148
feedback 128, 136, 148
feeling overwhelmed 8, 9, 17, 20, 21
finding your ONE THING 80-2
flexible schedule 126
focusing collective actions 11
focusing on what matters 155
frameworks and strategies 40-2
fun 129, 150

G

Garner, Helen 23
gathering players 141-2
getting ONE THING right 79-85
getting ONE THING wrong 75-8
getting underway 50
Godin, Seth 121
Goldsmith, Marshall 100

H

health costs from overwork 22

Heath, Dan and Chip 125
'how' of work 13, 150

I

identifying your ONE THING 70,
    80-2, 84, 90, 91
inability to identify what to do 35
inability to implement effectively 36
inability to make decisions 32
inability to prioritise 76
inclusion 58, 76
individual ONE THING 11
inertia 17, 76, 152
informing 112, 114
innovative environment 17
intended outcomes 155
involvement 112, 114

J

James, William 23
'Just do ONE THING' 7-10

K

keeping everyone on track 129
Keller, Gary 81
kick-arse level of deep 63-4
kick-arse message 124-6
knowing your market 123-4

L

latecomers 114
leaders/leadership team 94, 150
    accountability 95, 100-2
    celebrating achievements 104-5
    engagement and 114
    leading well 156
    level of ONE THING 11
    political campaign 88, 93-105
    reflection 104-5
    rewarding others 102
    support from 77, 84, 94
learning 128
Lencioni, Patrick 43
levels of ONE THING 11-12

list of things to improve on 14
listening 90, 91, 95-8, 102, 111, 122, 144
listening skills 144-5
listening tour 96-8, 139
living your ONE THING 100-1
long-term thinking 28-9

M

making time 80
management by walking around 97
marketing campaign 88, 119-31
    commitment 122
    content 128
    events 128
    everything speaking to same
    idea 121
    having fun 129
    knowing your market 123-4
    learning 128
    listening 122
    message 120, 123, 124-7, 130
    positive mindset 121
    resources 127
    schedule 126-7
    sticky message 120, 125-6
    testing ideas 128
    touchpoints 128
    working with sponsors 129
Mattea, Della 126
Mead, Margaret 116
meaningful involvement 84
meaningful ONE THING 54-5, 152
message 39, 90, 120, 146-7, 150
    clear 39, 90, 98-100, 120, 125,
    150, 153
    'Commander's Intent' 125
    marketing campaign 120, 122,
    124-7, 130
    political campaign 95, 98-100
    poll to decide on 146-7
    simple 120
    sticky 120, 125-6, 150
modelling 100, 101, 102
multiple perspectives 58

www.ingramcontent.com/pod-product-compliance
Lightning Source LLC
Chambersburg PA
CBHW060041030426
42334CB00019B/2435